Deep Sleep

Deep Sleep

Jim McJunkin

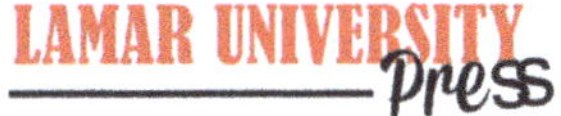

ISBN: 978-1-942956-04-4
Library of Congress Control Number: 2015938780

Manufactured in the United States
Photo Art: Jim McJunkin

Lamar University Press
Beaumont, Texas

For Beth

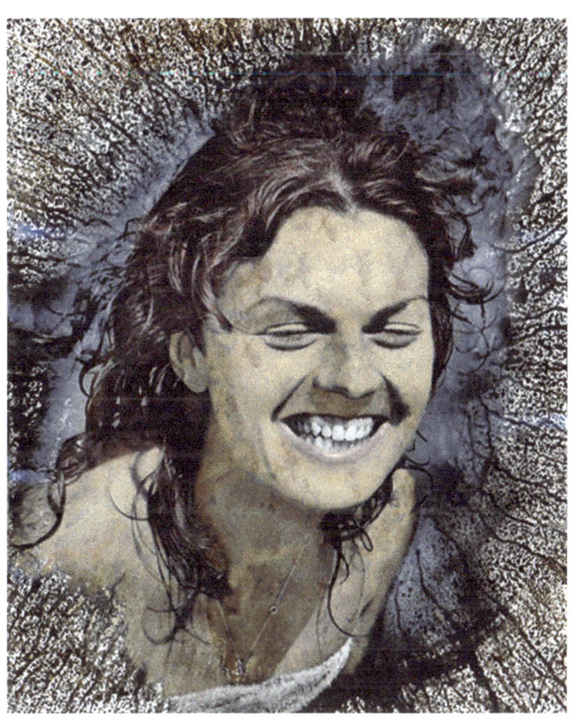

who listens to my dreams

Books from Lamar University Press

Jean Andrews, *High Tides, Low Tides: the Story of Leroy Colombo*
Charles Behlen, *Failing Heaven*
Alan Berecka, *With Our Baggage*
David Bowles, *Flower, Song, Dance: Aztec and Mayan Poetry*
Jerry Bradley, *Crownfeathers and Effigies*
Julie Chappell and Marilyn Robitaille, editors, *Writing Texas, 2013-14*
Terry Dalrymple, *Love Stories (Sort Of)*
Chip Dameron, *Waiting for an Etcher*
Robert Murray Davis, *Levels of Incompetence: An Academic Life*
William Virgil Davis, *The Bones Poems*
Jeffrey Delotto, *Voices Writ in Sand*
Gerald Duff, *Memphis Mojo*
Ted L. Estess, *Fishing Spirit Lake*
Mimi Ferebee, *Wildfires and Atmospheric Memories*
Ken Hada, *Margaritas and Redfish*
Michelle Hartman, *Disenchanted and Disgruntled*
Michelle Hartman, *Irony and Irreverence*
Katherine Hoerth, *Goddess Wears Cowboy Boots*
Lynn Hoggard, *Motherland, Stories and Poems from Louisiana*
Dominique Inge, *A Garden on the Brazos*
Gretchen Johnson, *The Joy of Deception*
Gretchen Johnson, *A Trip Through Downer, Minnesota*
Laozi, *The daodejing*, tr. David Breeden, Steven Schroeder, Wally Swist
Christopher Linforth, *When You Find Us We Will Be Gone*
Tom Mack and Andrew Geyer, editors, *A Shared Voice*
Dave Oliphant, *The Pilgrimage, Selected Poems: 1962-2012*
Janet McCann, *The Crone at the Casino*
Erin Murphy, *Ancilla*
Kornelijus Platelis, *Solitary Architectures*
Harold Raley, *Louisiana Rogue*
Carol Coffee Reposa, *Underground Musicians*
Carol Smallwood, *Water, Earth, Air, Fire, and Picket Fences*
Jim Sanderson, *Trashy Behavior*
Jim Sanderson, *Sanderson's Fiction Writing Manual*
Jan Seale, *Appearances*
Jan Seale, *The Parkinson Poems*
Glen Sorestad, *Hazards of Eden: Poems from the Southwest*
Melvin Sterne, *The Number You Have Reached*
John Wegner, *Love is Not a Dirty Word and Other Stories*
Robert Wexelblatt, *The Artist Wears Rough Clothing*
Jonas Zdanys, *Pushing the Envelope*

For more information about these and other books, go to
www.LamarUniversityPress.Org

Acknowledgments

I am greatly indebted to the following people. Without their assistance, the publication of this book would not have been possible: Carroll Wilson, editor for Lamar University Press; Nancy Scalise, who was a good sounding board for ideas; Don Minnick, navigator; Dan Gauthier; and Jerry Craven.

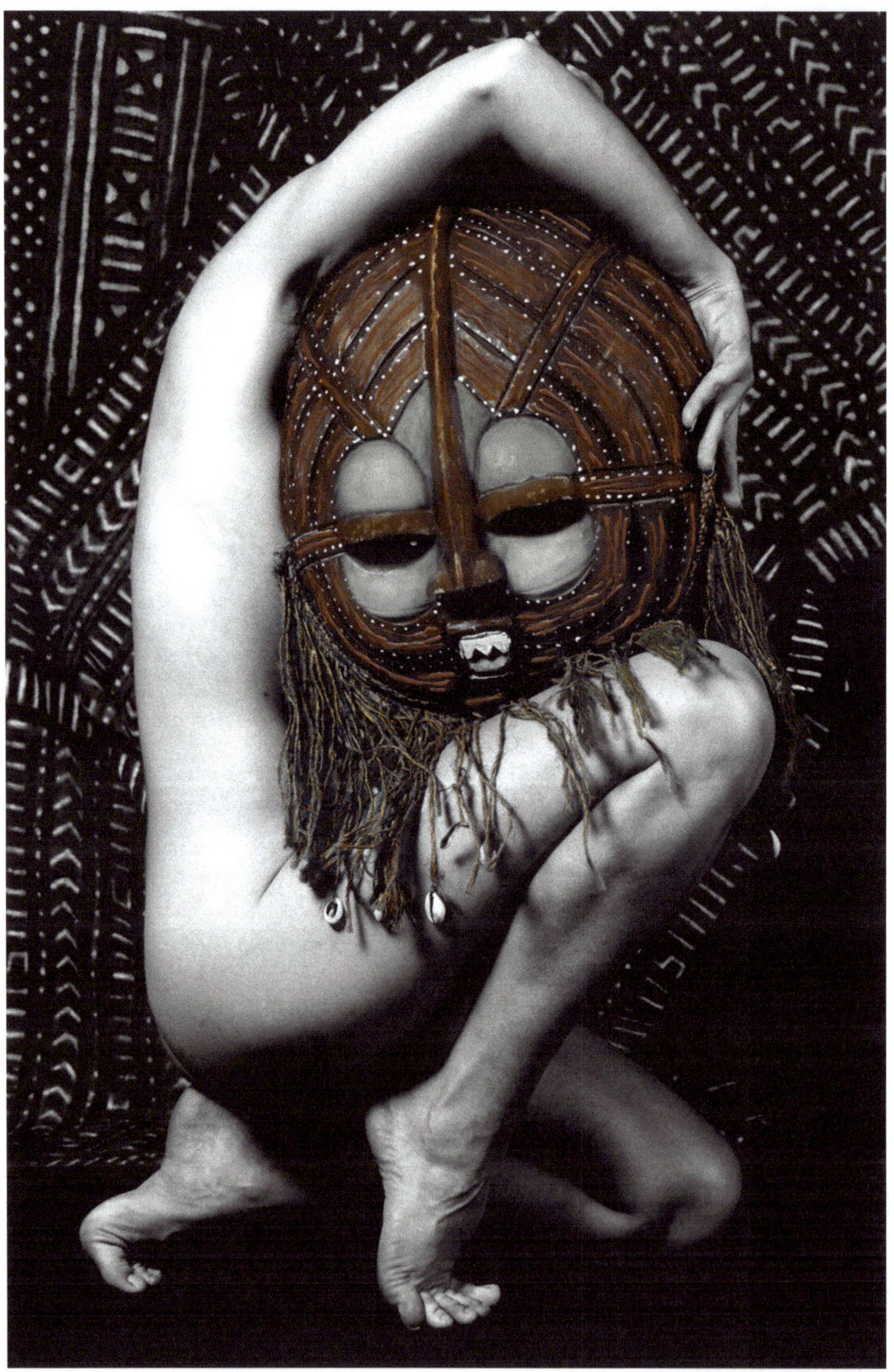

INTRODUCTION

Thanks to Facebook, Twitter, Instagram, Flickr, Tumblr, and other emerging social technologies, the content of conversations may be more about images and less about words in this decade of the 21st century.

One online service that tries to track such things suggested in mid-2013 that 300 million new photos were added to Facebook every day during 2012. Since its inception, the total number of photos uploaded to Instagram so far exceeds 5 billion. And at least fifty-eight photos are uploaded to Instagram every second.

Clearly everyone with a smart phone and who doesn't have one, regardless of age? uses it to take and send photographs, to "talk" with one another through visuals, to annotate all of life with photos of absolutely everything one encounters or, sometimes, just thinks about encountering.

Photography has become nothing if not banal, the act of producing pixilated gibberish.

It is one thing, however, to shoot snapshots with the latest Apple iPhone and post them to Facebook. It is another thing to, as journalists and other professionals do, capture images to tell stories or to use as illustrations for newspapers, magazines and books, perhaps to accompany and illuminate textual material or perhaps simply to stand alone as part of a more nuanced or studied discussion. But, it is an altogether different thing to take photos for a larger, more complex, more edifying purpose to take photos and use them as an art form.

Jim McJunkin's photographs belong in this realm. He shoots scenes, and then he changes them, some radically, some subtly, unless they meet strict personal criteria for what constitutes "documentation" (and very, very few do). In a word that has great traction in the wide world of professional photography, Jim manipulates photographs.

In that wide world, photo manipulation has something of a bruised reputation. The terms have for decades stood in the public mind for something bordering on fraud. That 1982 photograph of the Great Pyramids of Egypt that appeared on the cover of *National Geographic*, with one pyramid "moved" closer to another so as to fit better in the vertical format, comes to mind. The *TV Guide* cover photo of Oprah Winfrey's head obviously attached to the body of someone far slimmer is another example. *Time* magazine gave photo portraiture a bad name when it substantially darkened the cover photo of O.J. Simpson, notoriously freed after a lengthy murder trial, back in 1994. Political operatives went back into the news image archives of the 1970s to pull together two different pictures in an ultimately aborted effort to make John Kerry, who was running for the office of president in 2004, look bad. One picture was of then-excoriated Jane Fonda, and one was of then-ex-combatant-turned-peace-activist John Kerry. And in May 2013, the fashion editors of *The New York Times* were called on the carpet for removing the tattoo from a woman modeling clothes.

In fact, the discussion of photo manipulation was broadened and enriched in 2012 when The Metropolitan Museum of Art in New York City opened a major exhibit featuring the history of doctored images. The works dated back to the first years of photography.

An adjunct show also opened in 2012 at the Met called "After Photoshop: Manipulated Photography in the Digital Age," and it is to be suspected that while the main exhibit focused on the works that had been altered in the past, the real point of the Met's efforts was to point out how easy it is to distort that which is "real" by using Adobe Photoshop, the computer program that is the gold standard when it comes to dealing with photographs that are produced digitally rather than only on film.

Even though Photoshop has made it easy to manipulate photographs, it has not made it easier to produce an image that could be classified as fine art. That takes something called talent, as acknowledged by the Met in its choice of contemporary works to feature in the "After Photoshop" exhibit, and as underscored by the Center for Fine Art Photography in Fort Collins, Colorado, which in 2013 was featuring Photoshopped works by, among others, Susan Burnstine, whose images are, like Jim's, on the surrealistic end of the spectrum.

To create art with photographs is to enter a rarified environment, and it is there that Jim McJunkin's works, featured in this volume, fit very comfortably.

Entering that field, though, has taken Jim a while.

His initial artistic ambition was to paint, using oil on canvas. But, he had trouble imagining subject matter, and so he bought a 35-mm Minolta to capture images that he could than paint. At a couple of universities during the 1960s he tried to become an artist with paintbrush and oils, but he admits that he was not a very good student. In Denver toward the end of that decade he found himself taking his camera to anti-war demonstrations where he could hang out and shoot photos. He could be part of the action but also stand apart from it, unconsciously taking the artistic view of the reality that unfolded before his lens.

In 1969, under pressure from the local draft board, Jim signed up for two years of duty in the Army, thinking that by volunteering he would stay off the list of soldiers heading to Vietnam. At the recruiting station, he told the sergeant he was a professional photographer. As luck would have it, Jim did wind up in Vietnam not to wield an M-16 but instead a heavy, cumbersome 4x5 Speed Grafflex camera, which he later traded for a 35-mm version.

In Vietnam, he further refined his documentary sensibility, and to this day his favorite photos are still black-and-white records of real life.

From his experiences in Vietnam, Jim pulled pictures for a book he co-authored called *Visions of Vietnam*, published by Presidio Press, and for another collection called *Reflexes and Reflections*, published for the National Vietnam Veterans Art Group by Abrams.

Over time, though, Jim pushed against the limits of that kind of photography and began to see where he could go by using film as its own kind of canvas. In pre-digital times, he would scratch his negatives or apply paint to produce images that reflected his unique vision.

"So," Jim says, "I have this dichotomy of images, documentary versus embellished, black-and-white versus color, real versus not real. The only world in which such images exist side-by-side is mental, and so I hit upon the idea of a collection of dream images."

Jim has an active dream life, and he avidly writes down descriptions of those dreams.

The evidence presented here indicates that his dreams seem to be based on anything but reality. Some of the images are disturbing, bordering on nightmarish. Others are simply visually arresting. The result of Jim's dreams and the images he keeps in his head and sometimes commits to photographic paper is this book. *Deep Sleep*, like his dreams themselves, is where fact and fiction merge.

Indeed, it is tempting to call what he does in this volume "poetry."

Carroll Wilson
Wimberley, Texas

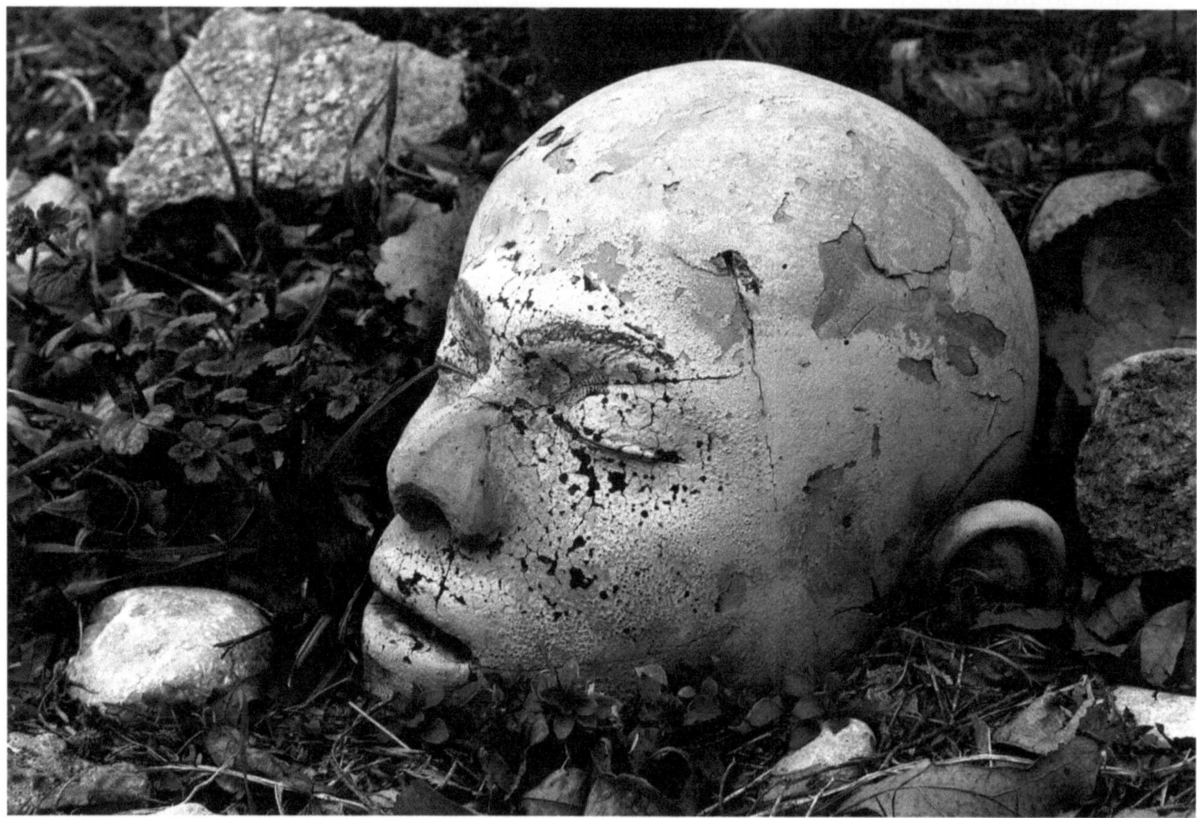

One night, I dreamed I took my head off and set it down to think about some things that were bothering me. It was an impulsive move, but not as bizarre as it sounds, given the deep animated sleep I was experiencing at the time.

But, the separation of mind and body proved to be more of a distraction than a path toward lucid thought. Without a neck to swivel on, my torso was just out of sight, and I worried about whether it was still there. Then I began to wonder what it might look like with another head, and how my head might appear on another body.

After some time and a good deal of concentration, those worries receded, and I realized that limited vision made it easier to view my past, which is where the things that were haunting me resided.

Personal history is the foundation of a dream, so I delved deep into my memory and saw alternate versions of the things I remembered. It was crowded and chaotic. The first people I met were caricatures of the real me who seemed to represent my feminine side, as well as some other aspects of my personality. Concerned and Amused were two distinct parts of the single entity that was me. They were the gatekeepers of my mind, and they shared an environmental landscape of fact and fiction.

Concerned warned me of the anguish and despair I would face should I continue.

"Go for it. Enjoy yourself," Amused said. "Everything in here is you, or of your creation. Nothing is new, except the way it is thrown back at you, distorted and out of context. It could be entertaining if you don't take it too seriously."

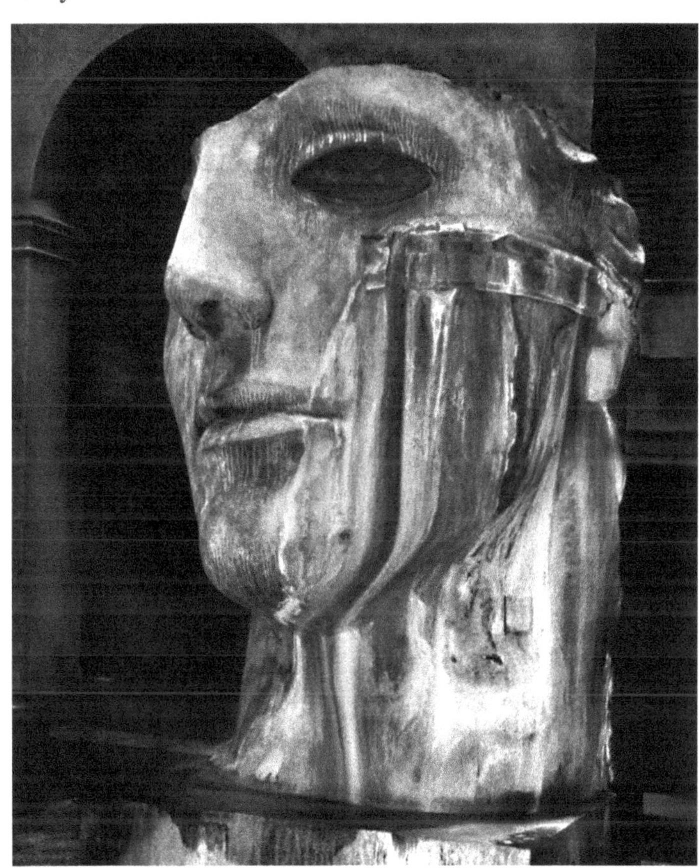

Amused was more persuasive, and I decided to follow her counsel. I was swayed by the thing she said about my present situation being nothing more than a dream about what was going on in my mind while I was not paying attention. "You should be more aware of this stuff", she said. "Anyway, it's just a dream, so what do you have to lose?"

Concerned was mumbling something about "my mind, and my future, and everything important in Life," but I was already moving inward, towards something I vaguely remembered.

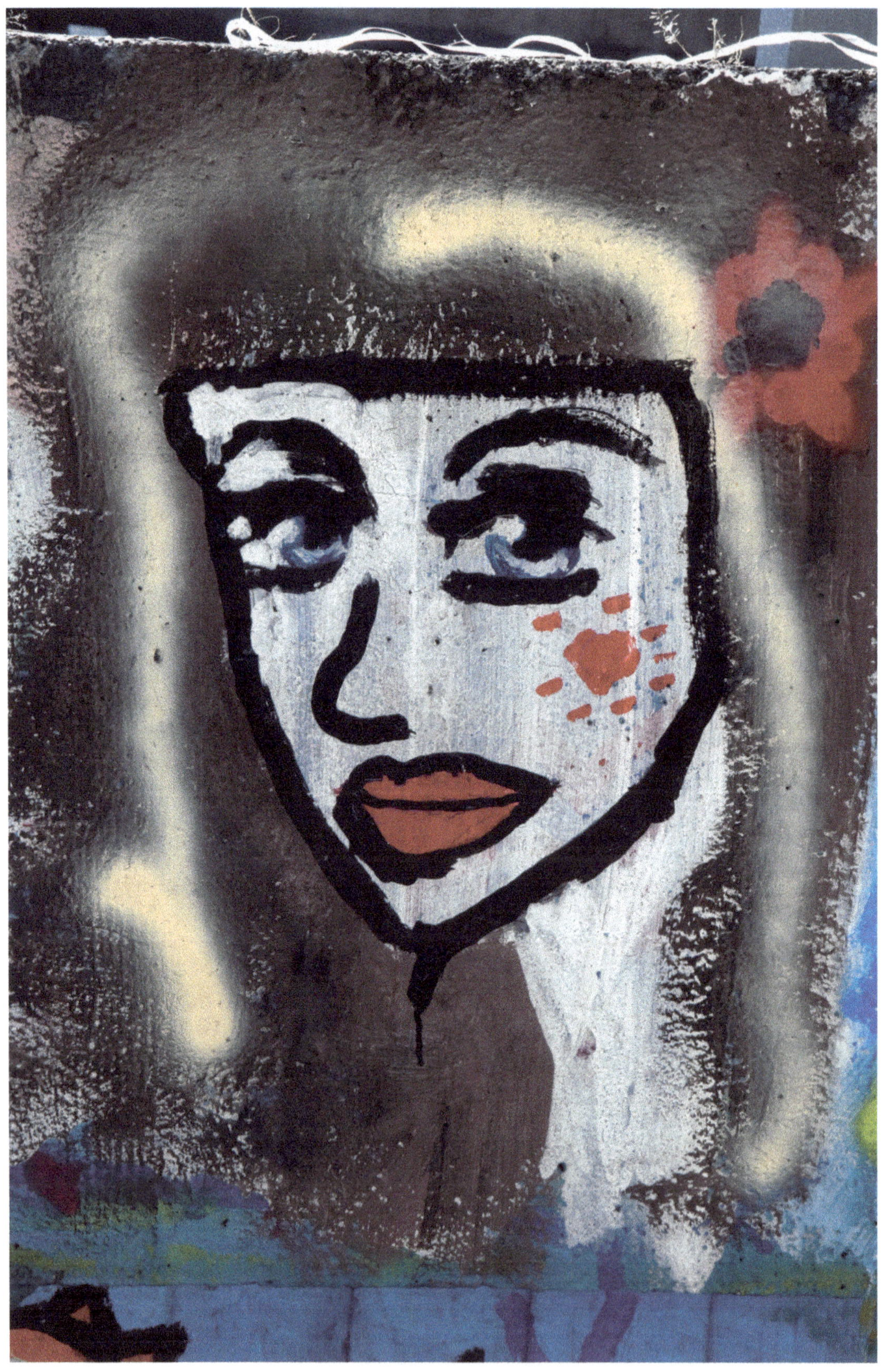

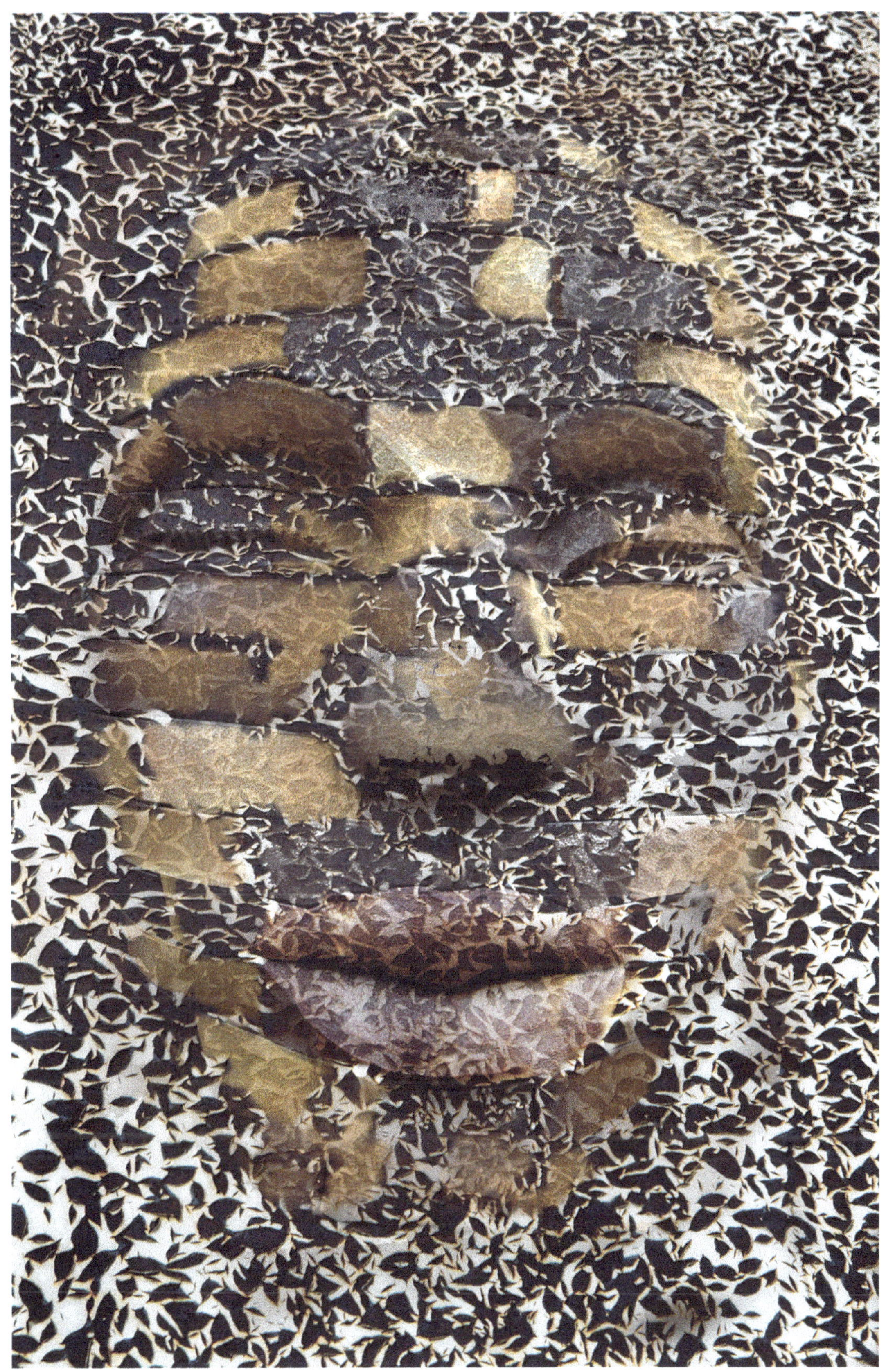

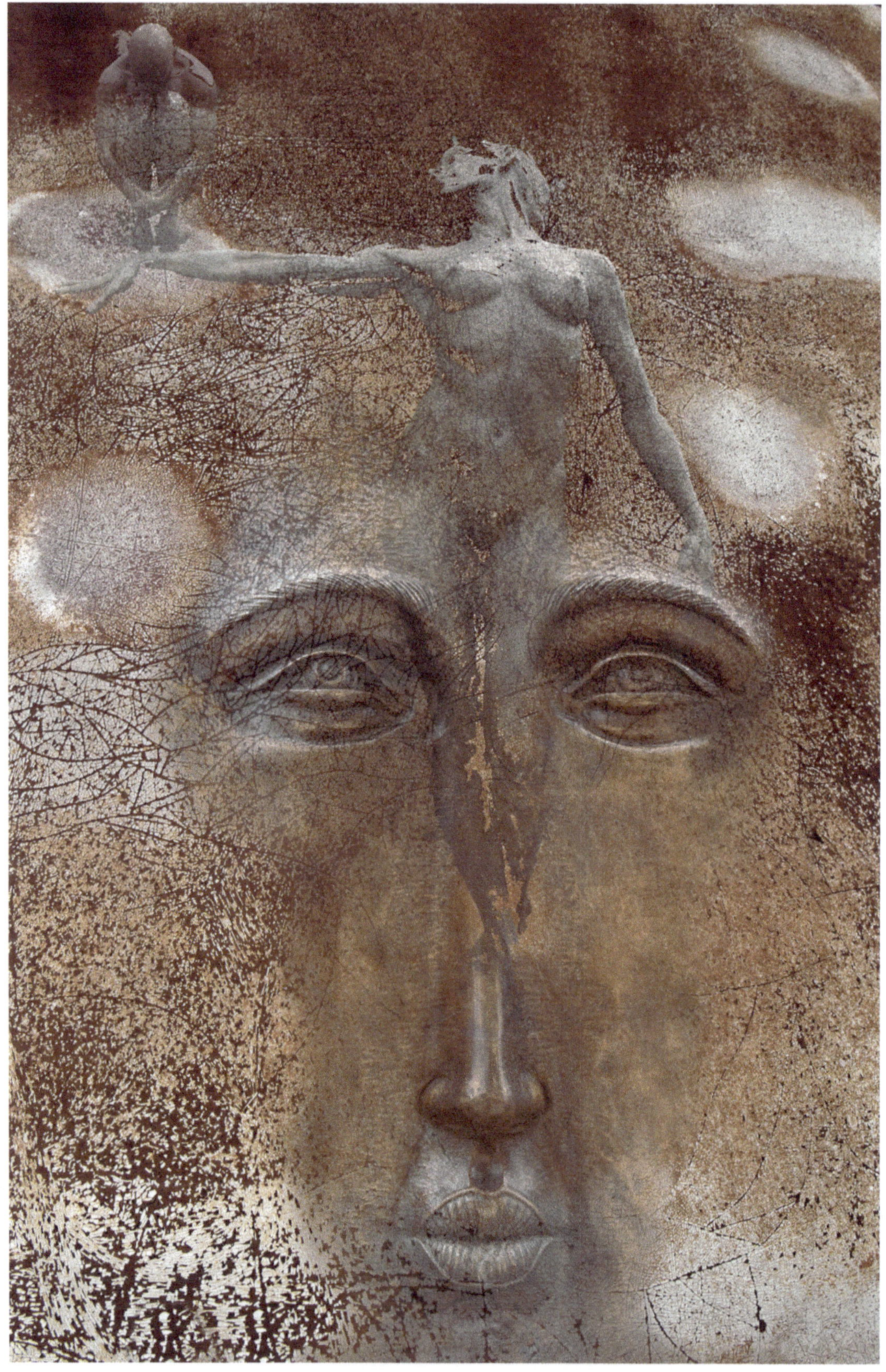

Real time progressed and my routine continued its comfortable rhythm of waking, dealing with life, going to sleep, and dreaming. Although I never saw Concerned and Amused again, my dreams were a continuation of that encounter. The gatekeepers had admitted me to a nightly performance of a re-creation of my past.

Old friends and familiar characters inhabited distorted versions of places I had visited while awake. I had to remind myself that they were not a collection of muscle and bone and earth. They were less than air. Everything I encountered was the result of electrical impulses and brain synapses that created the thought that built the world I was passing through. If I were real, I could put my finger right through it.

Many of those experiences roused my emotions. Lust and fear intermingled with boredom. I recall laughing in my sleep, and once I woke up crying.

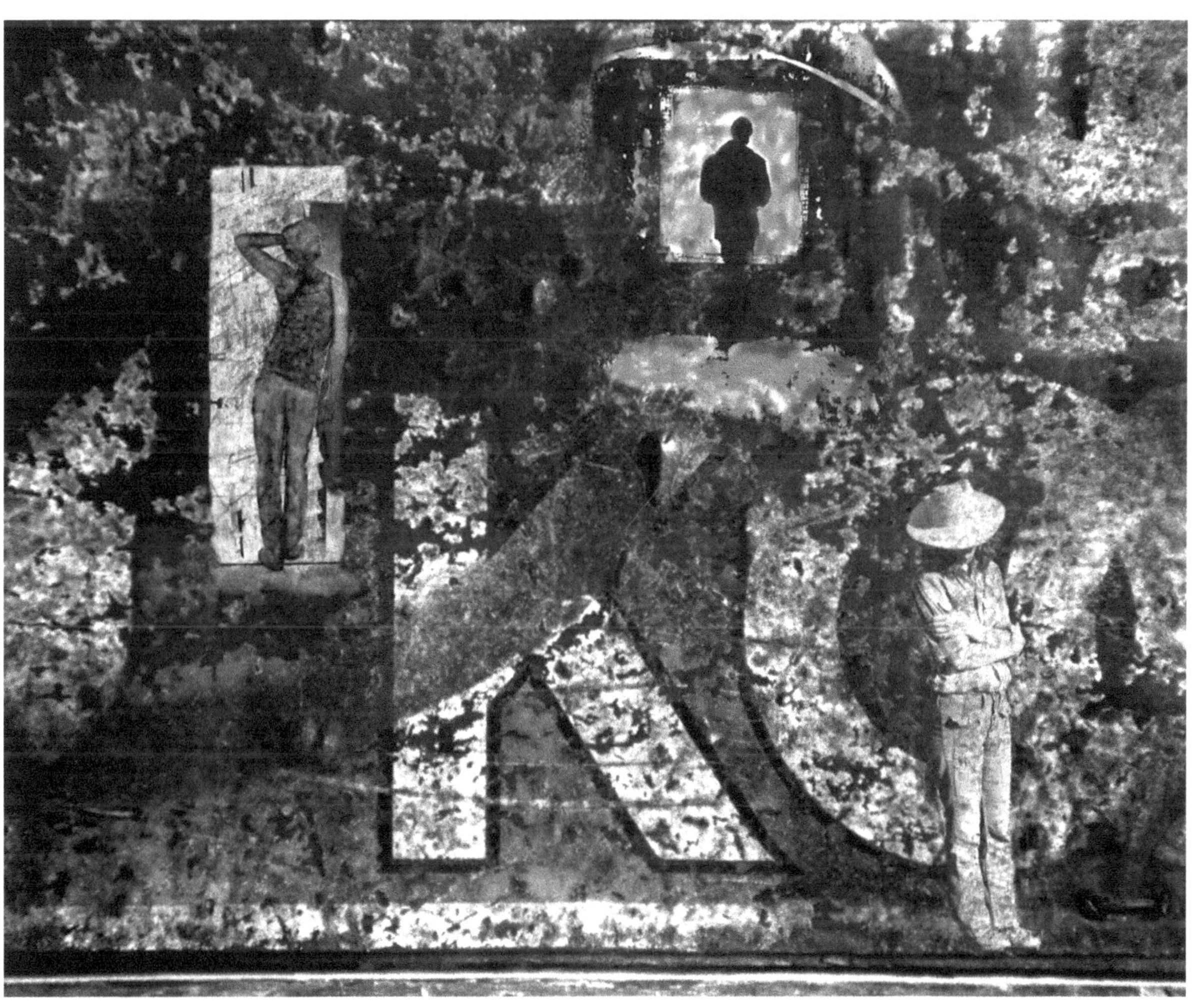

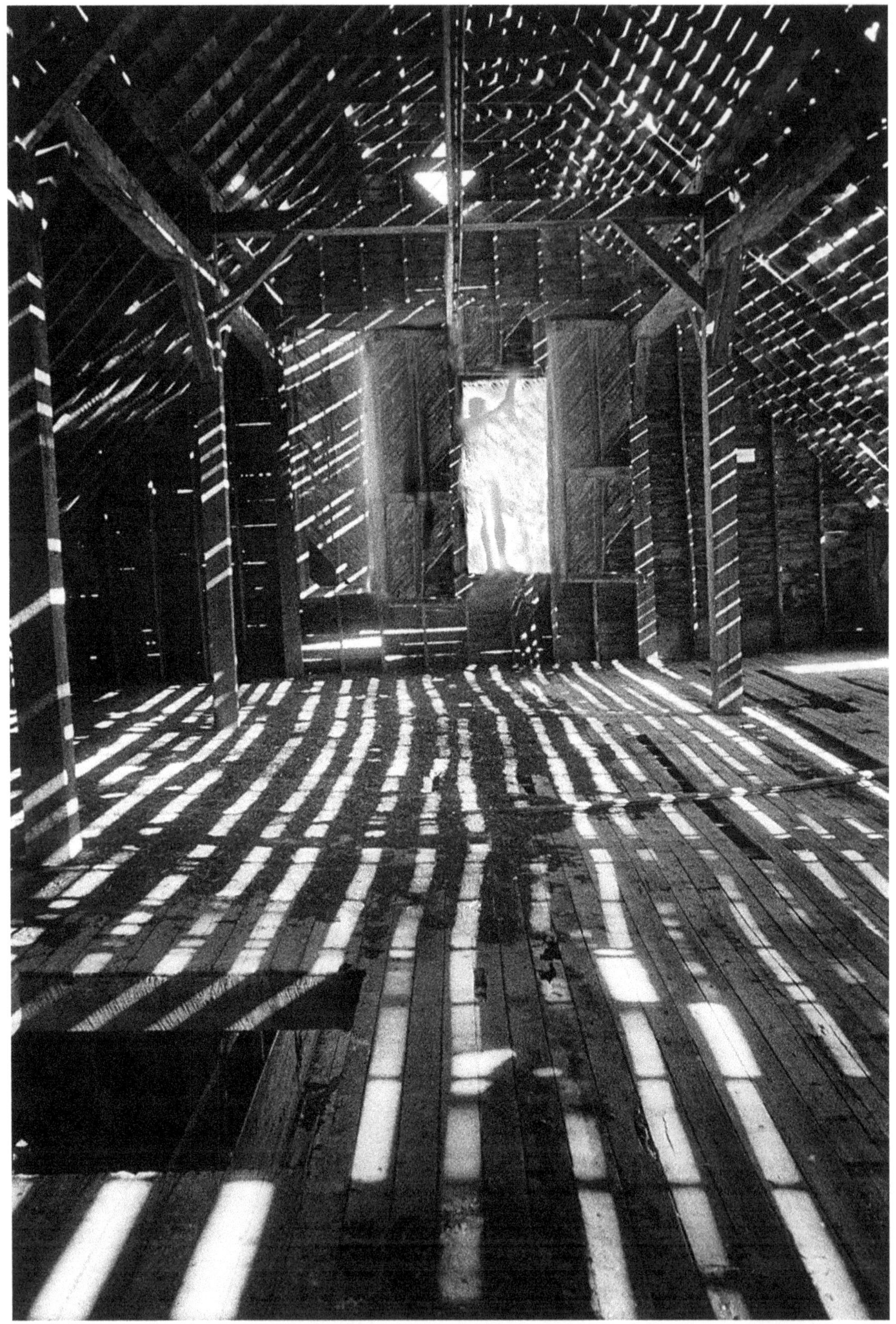

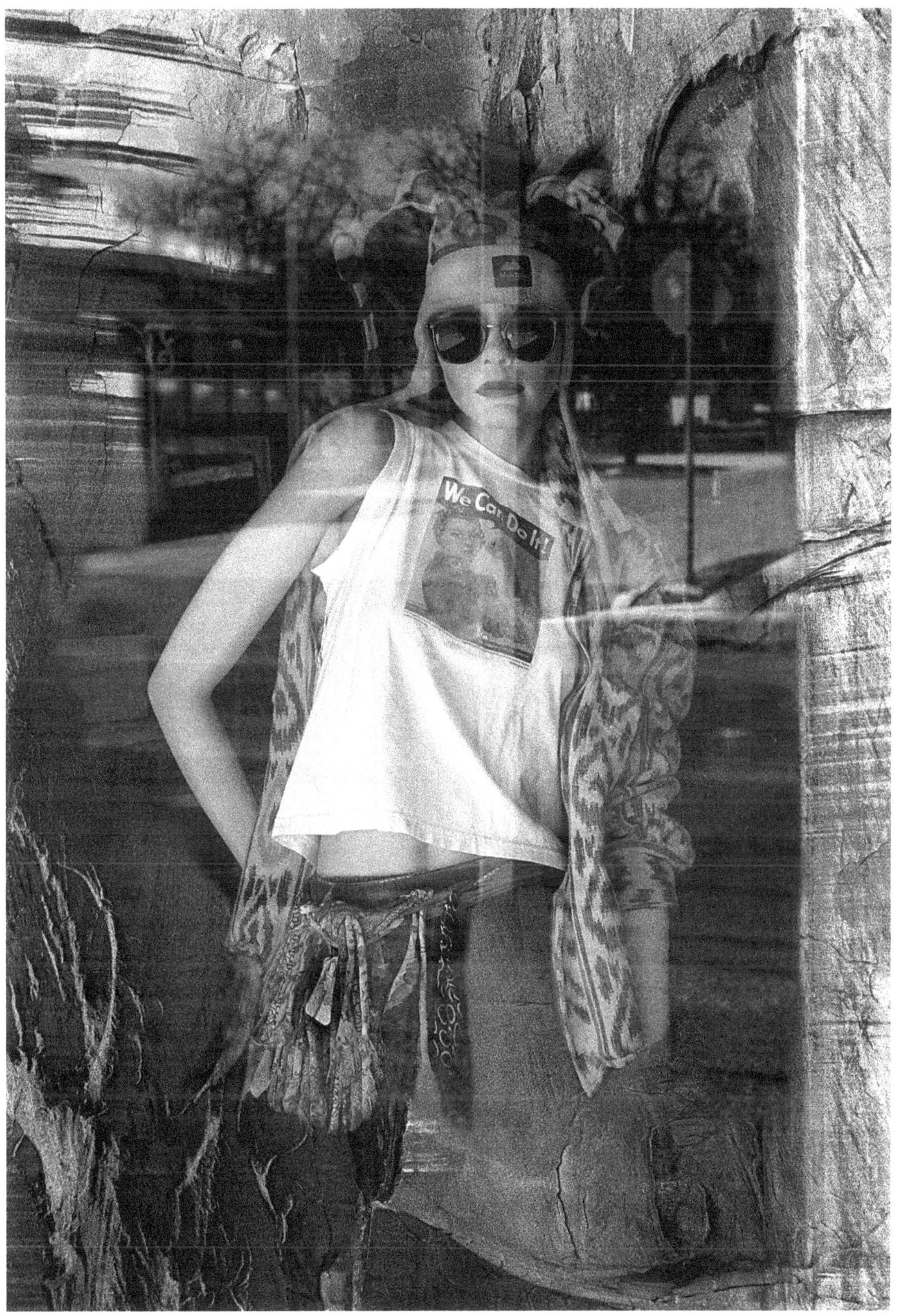
We Can Do It!

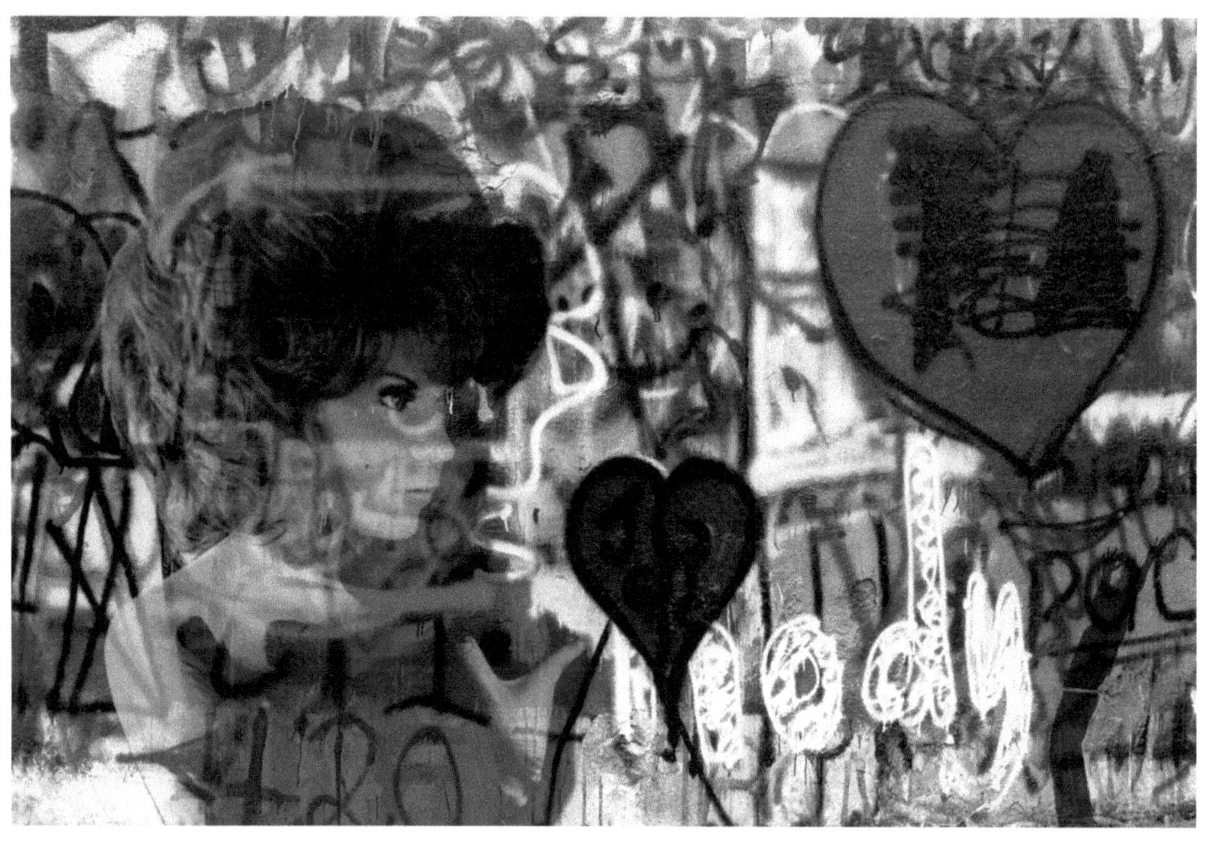

The earliest dream I can recall took place in Okinawa , where my family lived from the time I was five to nine years of age. In the dream I was in the jungle with friends. We came upon a clearing and discovered a burial casket on top of a stone slab. The sides of the casket were so high we had to stand on tiptoes to look inside.

I had a fearful premonition and told my friends not to look into the crypt because it would make their teeth melt. They peeked, of course, and I had to watch as they tried to scream, but all that came out of their mouths was a stream of enamel.

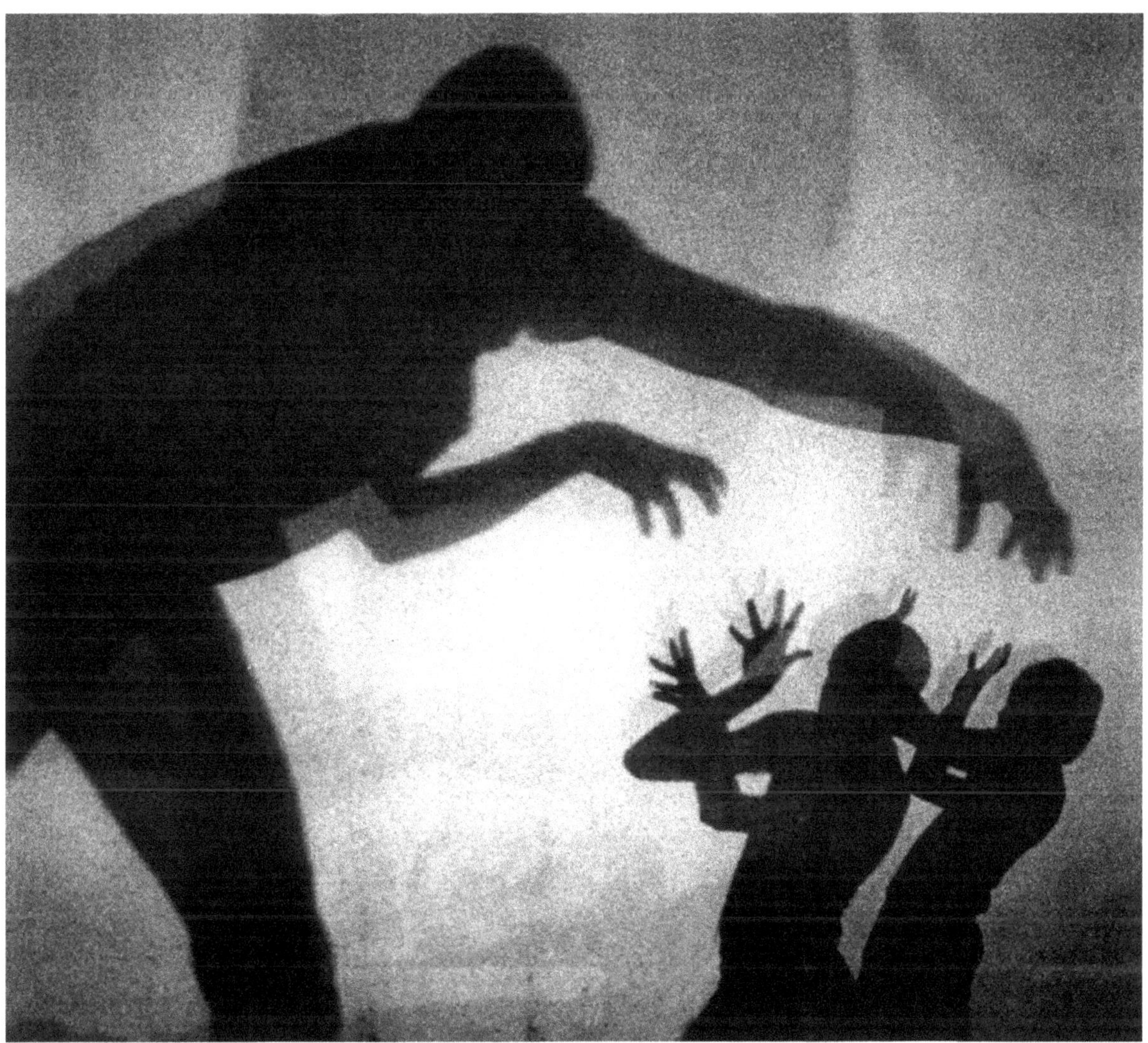

Growing up in Okinawa I was warned about the dangers of the jungle, unexploded ordnance left over from World War II and poisonous snakes, chief among them. And it was an easy place to become disoriented and lost.

I did manage to breach the fringes of that forbidden zone without being harmed or caught, but I do not recall seeing a burial crypt in real life. Still, the melting teeth nightmare was a recurring dream and stuck with me long after our family moved back to the United States. It was my most frightening dream until I was old enough to be drafted into the Army.

As I grow older, my dreams have become more violent, but less scary. The source of that violence has less to do with what I have experienced in life than what I have heard, read, or seen on television.

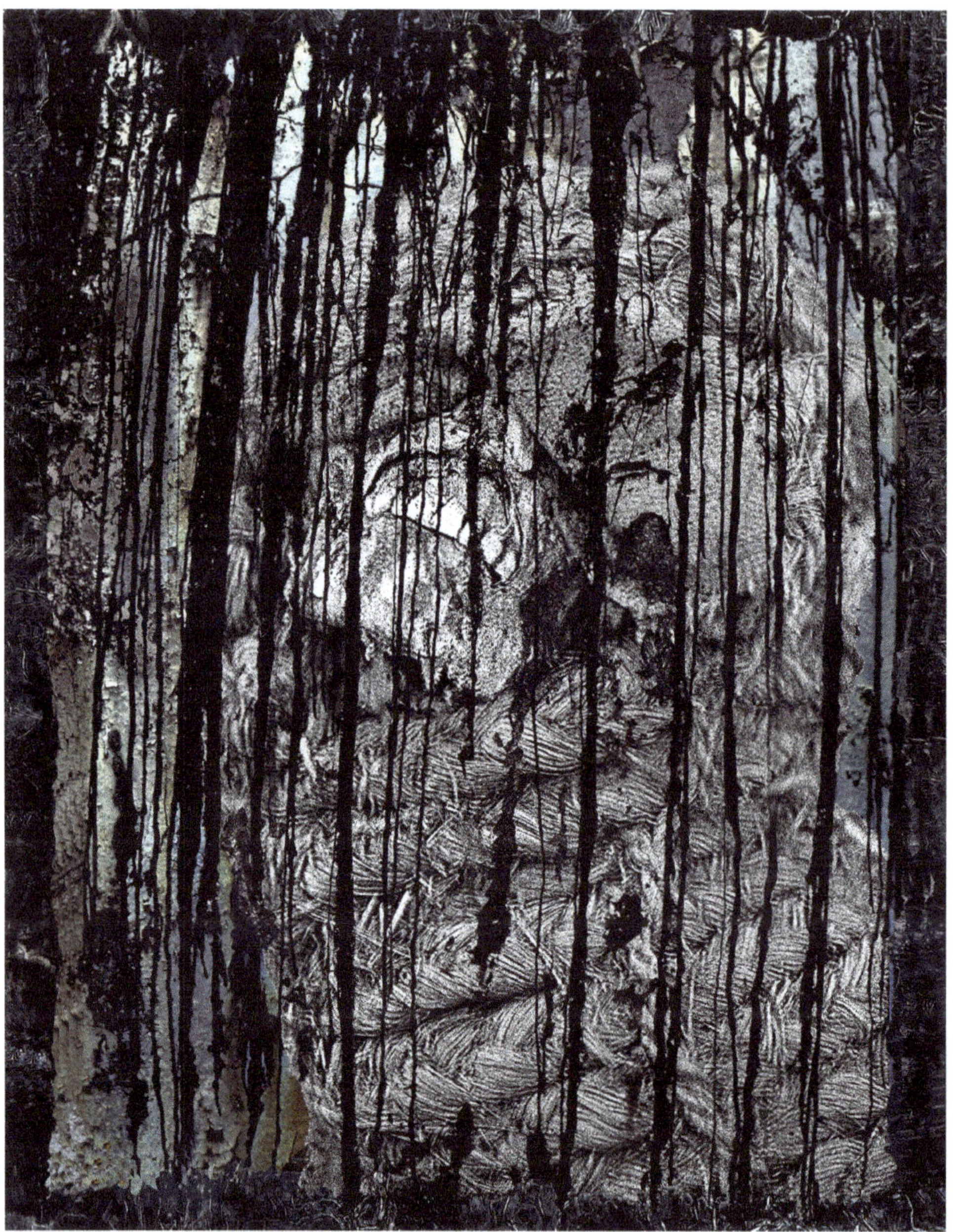

Dream violence surpasses everything I have experienced while awake. During sleep I am occasionally chased by people or creatures that are trying to kill me. Alarmingly, I have seen severed heads and stabbed people and experienced a good deal of blood and gore. Thankfully, though, I am now able to detach myself from the terror. Dream violence no longer bothers me enough to jar me awake.

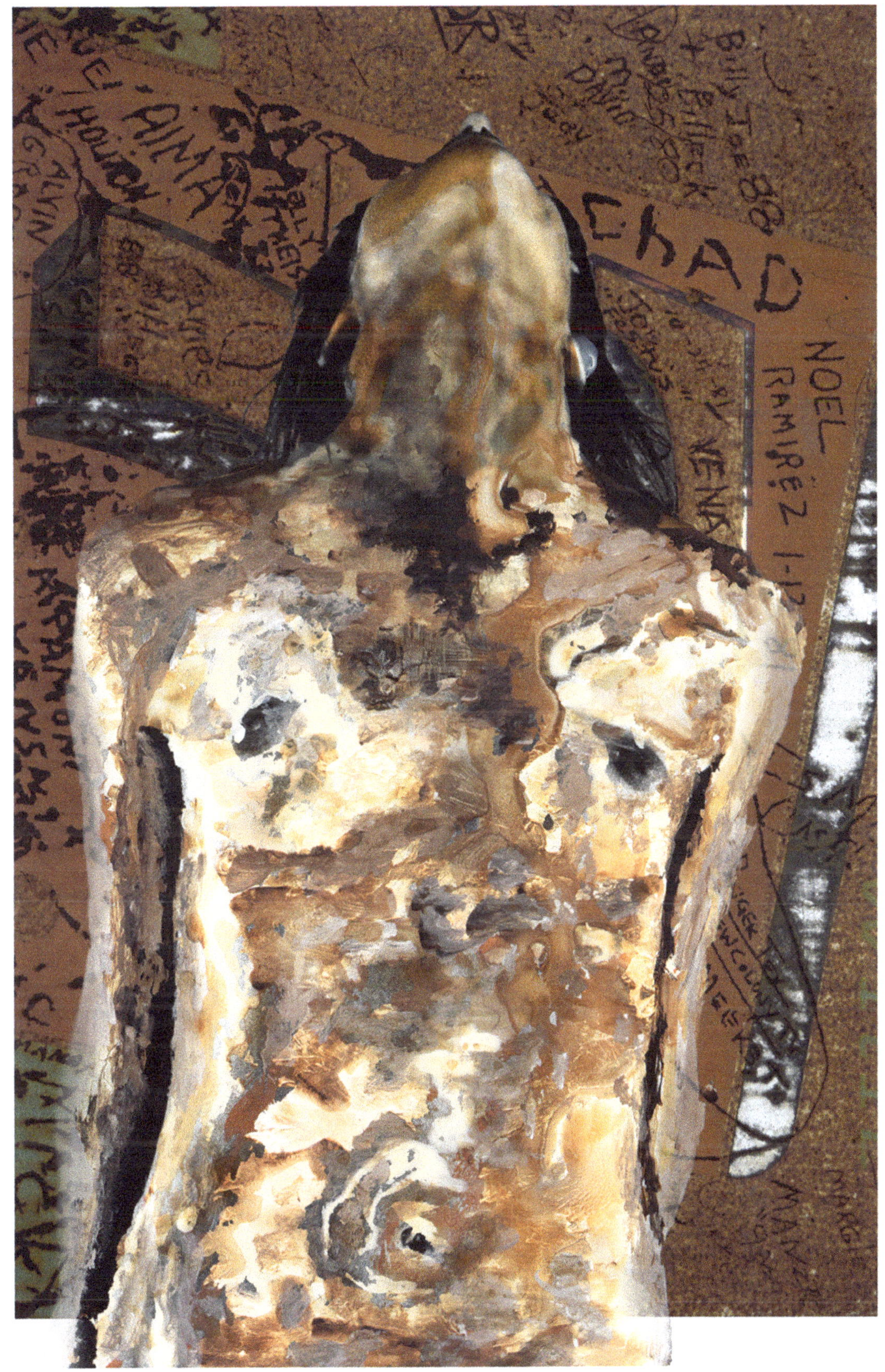
CHAD
NOEL
RAMIREZ

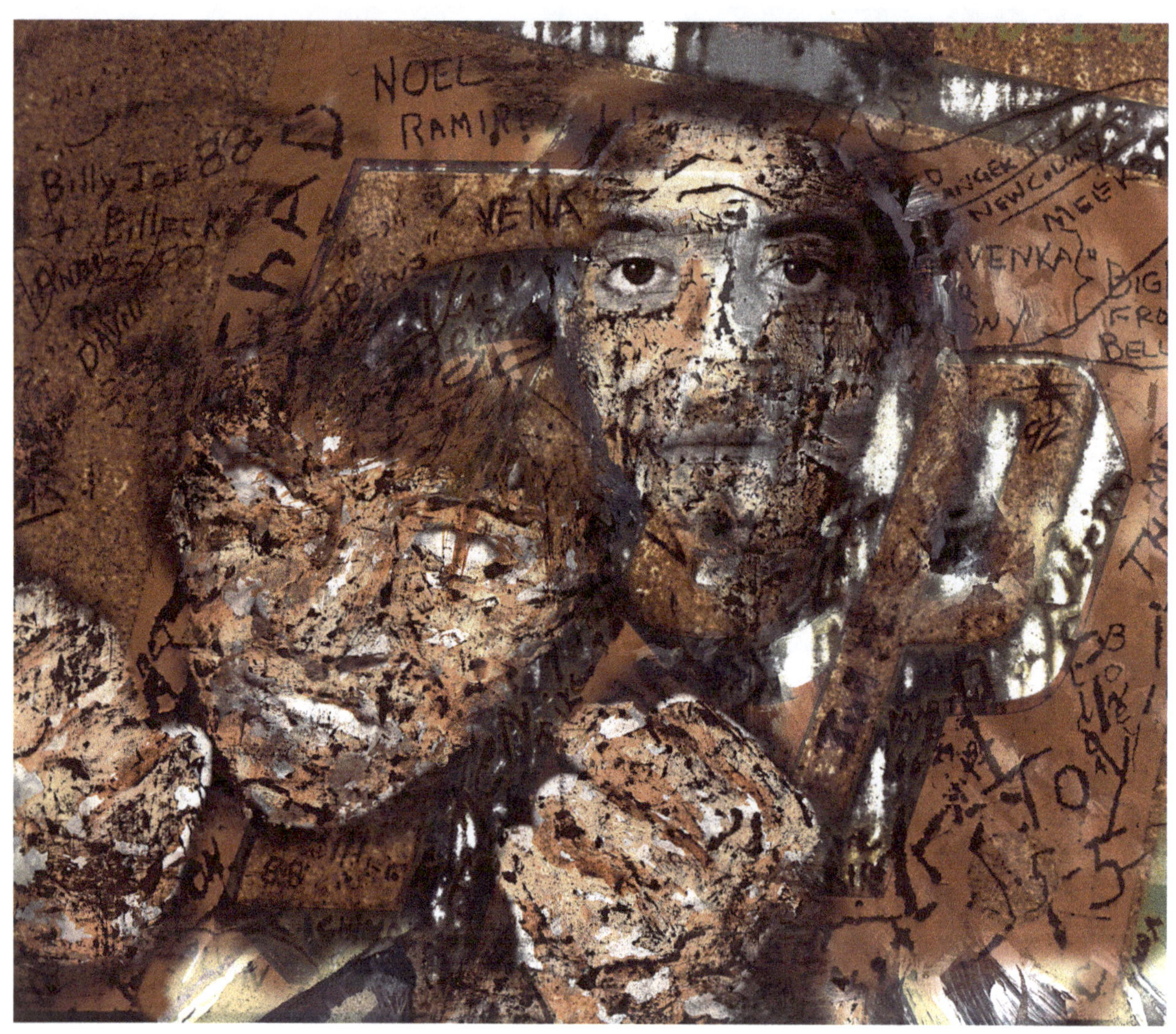
NOEL
Billy Joe 88
VENA
VENKA

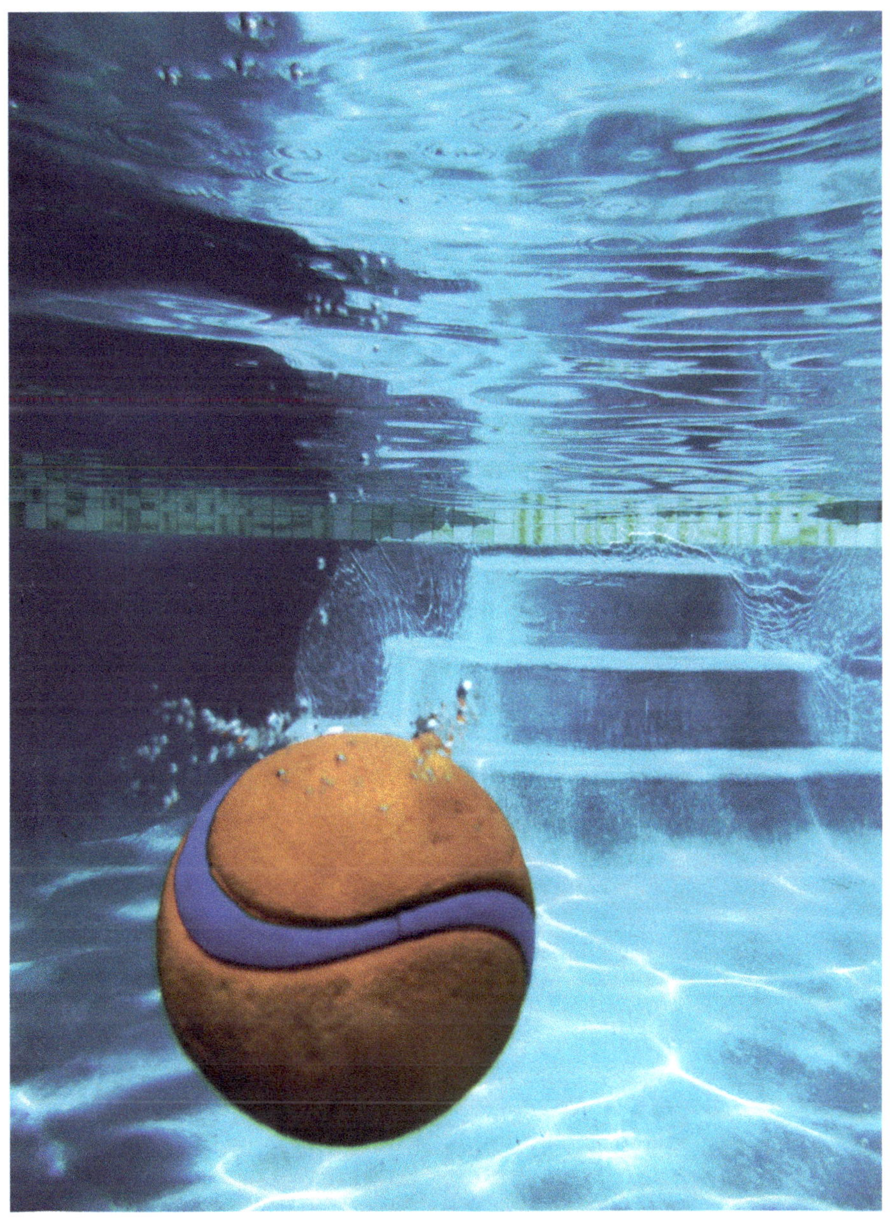

My Labrador retriever, whose thoughts seldom stray from ball chasing, swimming, and running, obsesses about those activities when she dreams. She sleeps excessively, and her body movements mimic what she does during slumber. As expected, her eyelids twitch during REM activity, and her paw movements are a sure indication of dream running. When she dream runs, her paws move rhythmically, barely touching the softly cushioned landscape of her mind. When she dream swims, her movements are less coordinated. Her feet pull inward, in a scooping motion, and her knuckles spread in an effort to produce more thrust in what her mind is telling her is a liquid environment. She is an athlete, able to progress through anything.

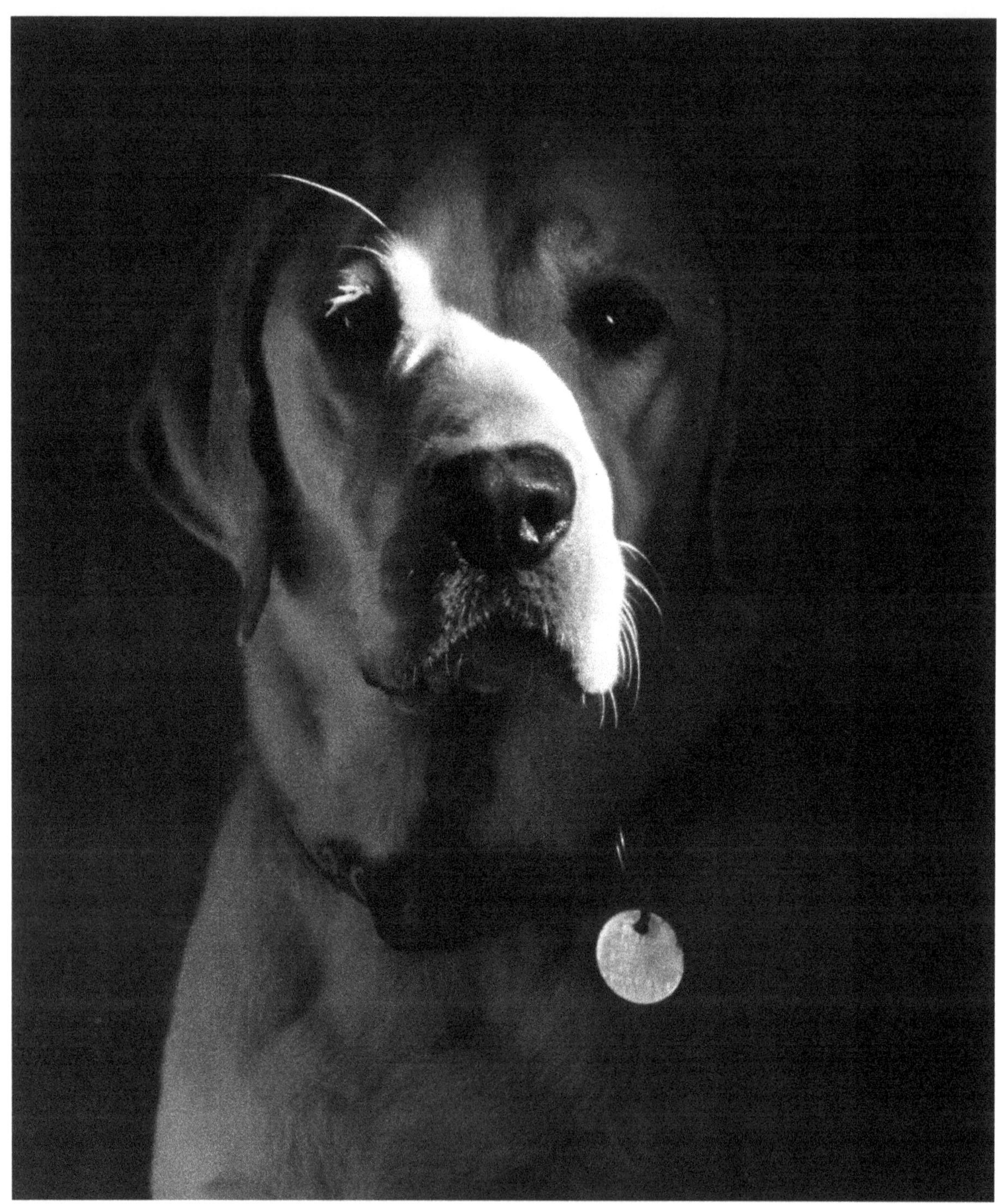

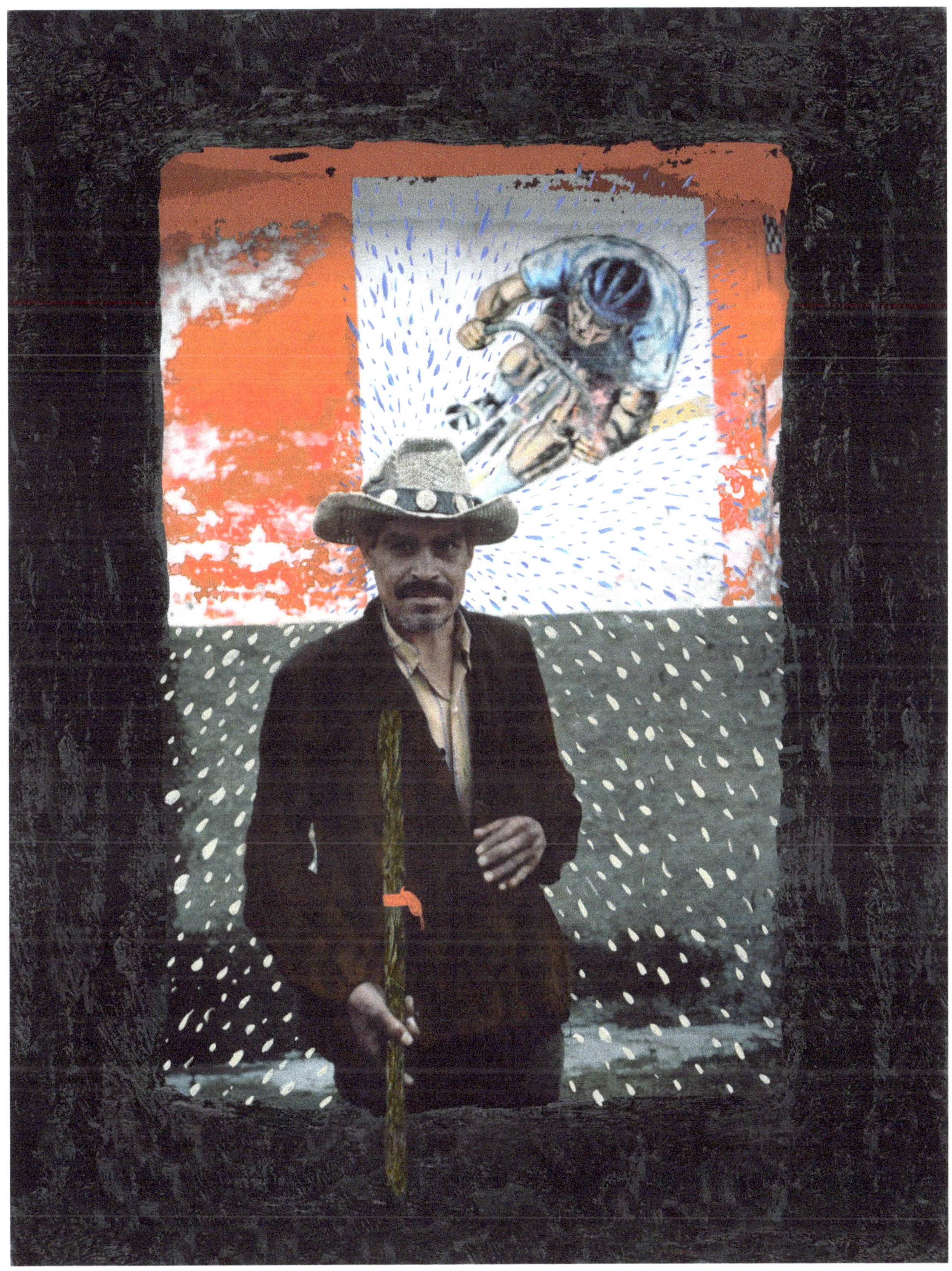

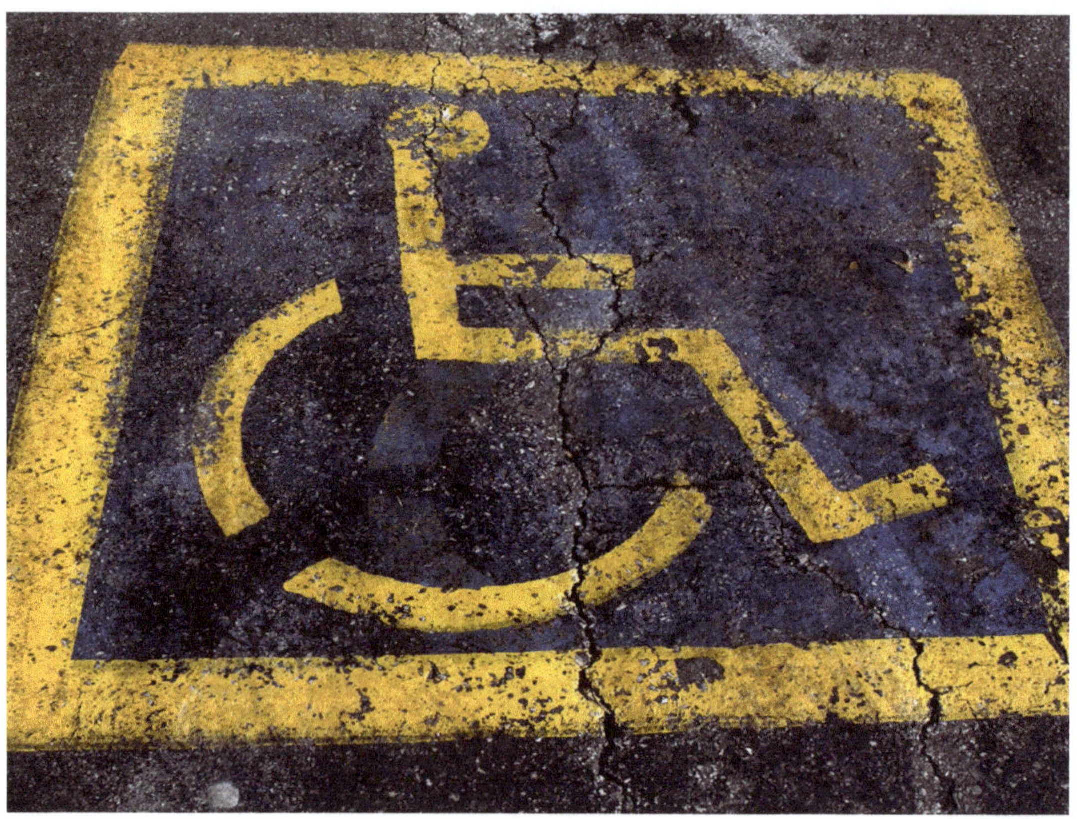

My dreams usually do not have sequels, but one particular episode led me to a fitful night of semi-related visualizations.

I was talking to a man in a Mexican village, asking directions to a place I needed to find. He said he could take me there and show me the magic stick that could make this possible.

At first I thought the man might be a shaman, some sort of magician, because everything around us began to move. All objects were drawn towards the stick, including me, and I became the man with the power, but I did not know how to wield it. I was acutely aware that the poster of a bicyclist behind me was gaining momentum.

I'm not sure if the impact woke me momentarily, or hurled me into another dream, but after the bicycle accident everything became animated, and I entered a cartoon world.

My world took on three dimensions, but it was compressed to the point where it almost lost depth. That was just fine with me since there are fewer places for bad things to hide in an almost two-dimensional world. Also, the place had a non-threatening, comic strip vibe that became even more comfortable as I adjusted by becoming somewhat more cartoonish myself. I have been many things in my dreams, not all of them human, so slowly devolving into a stick figure was no surprise. In fact, it was a comfortable fit for my surroundings.

I was on my way to someplace special and had a sense of anticipation about the trip. Travel became effortless, and I began to relax as a vast wasteland of backdrops slid past my vision.

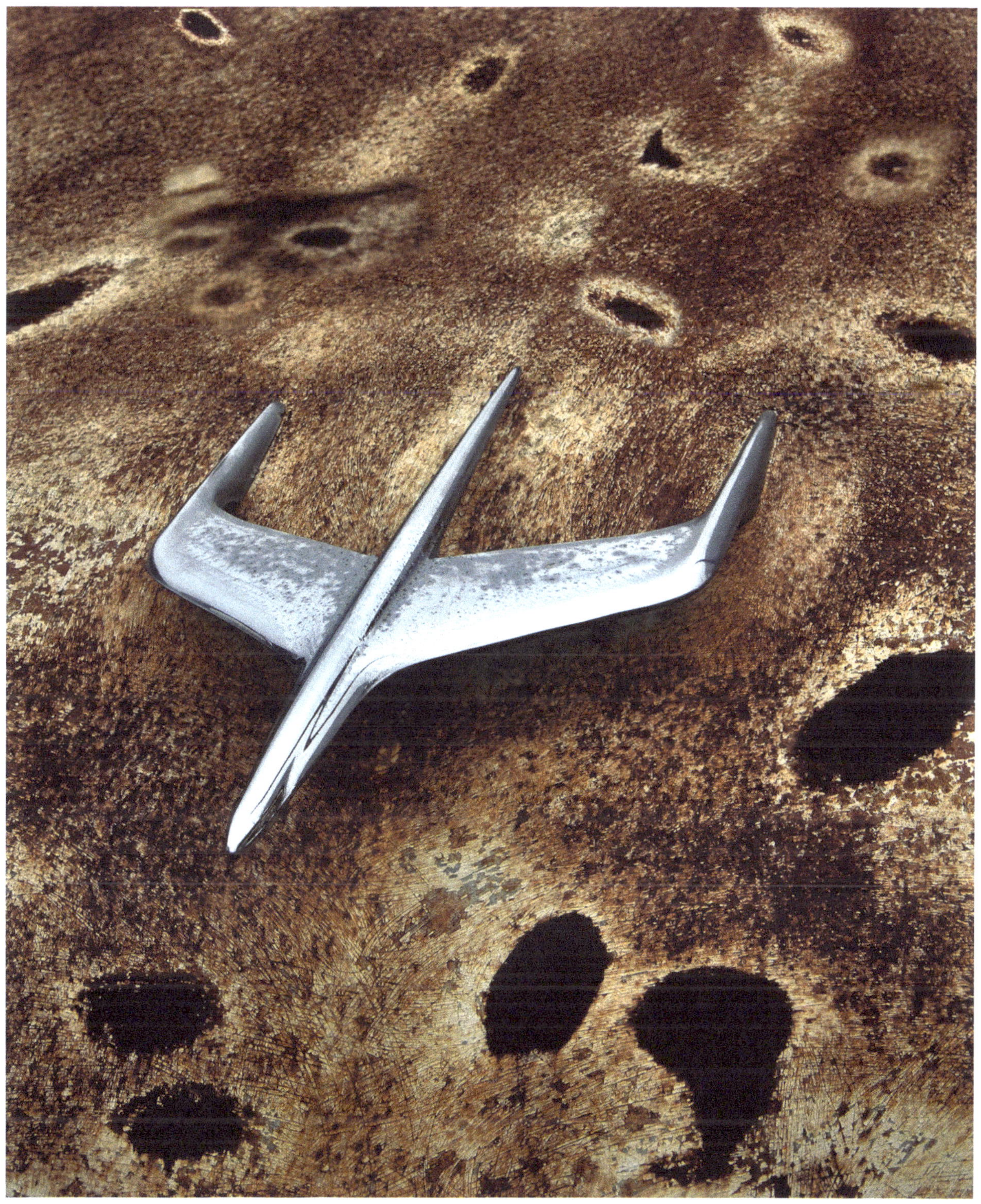

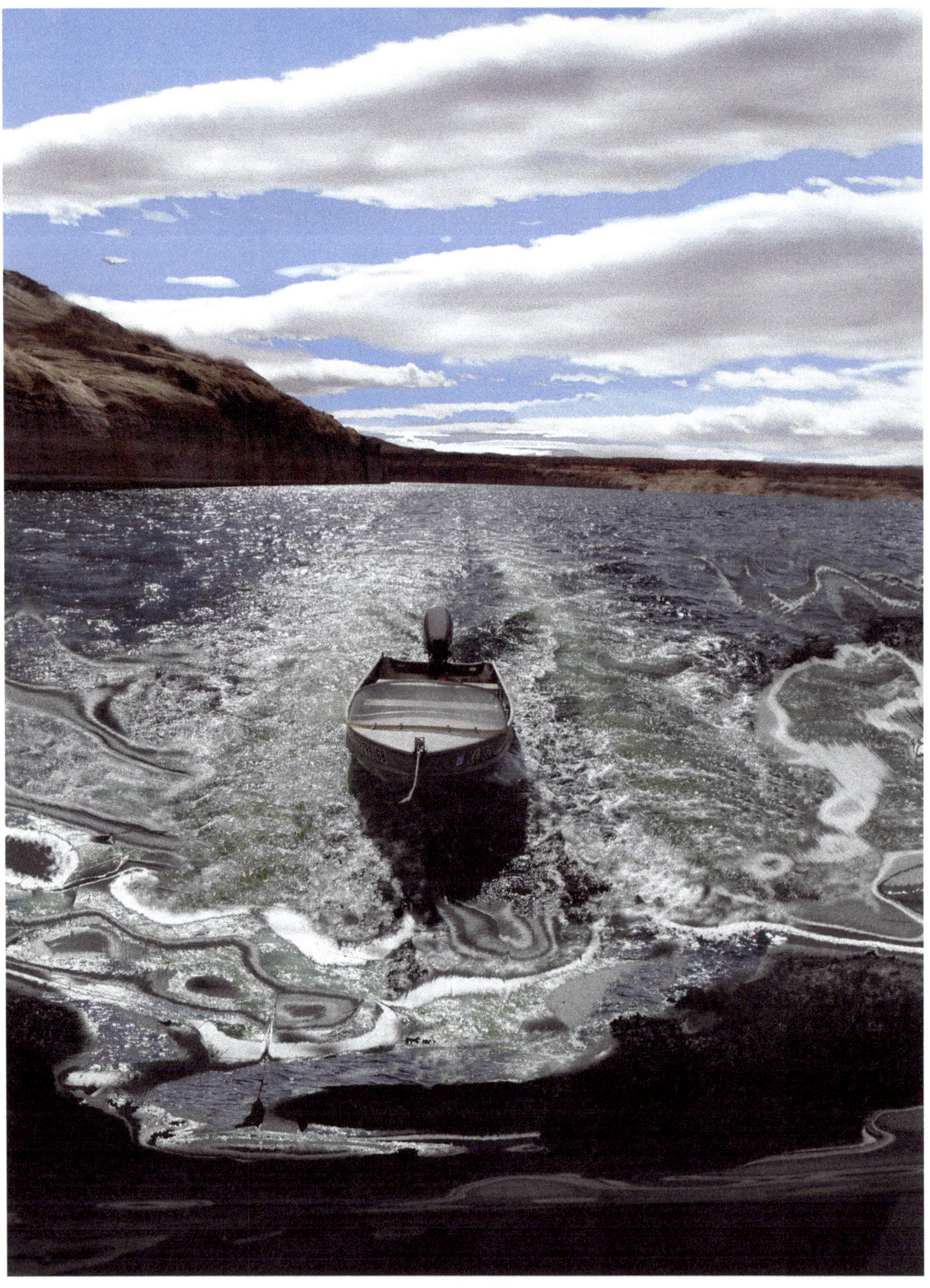

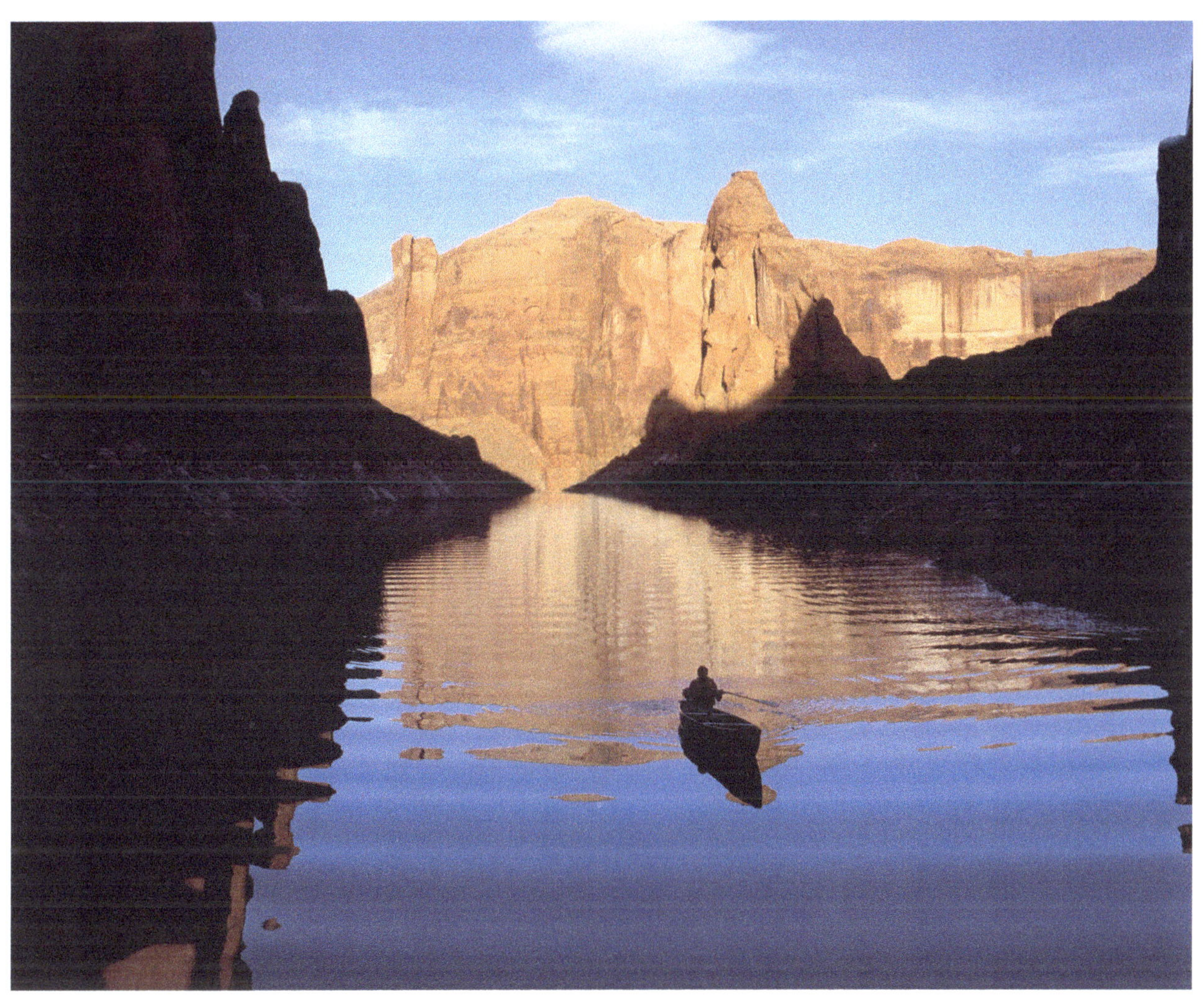

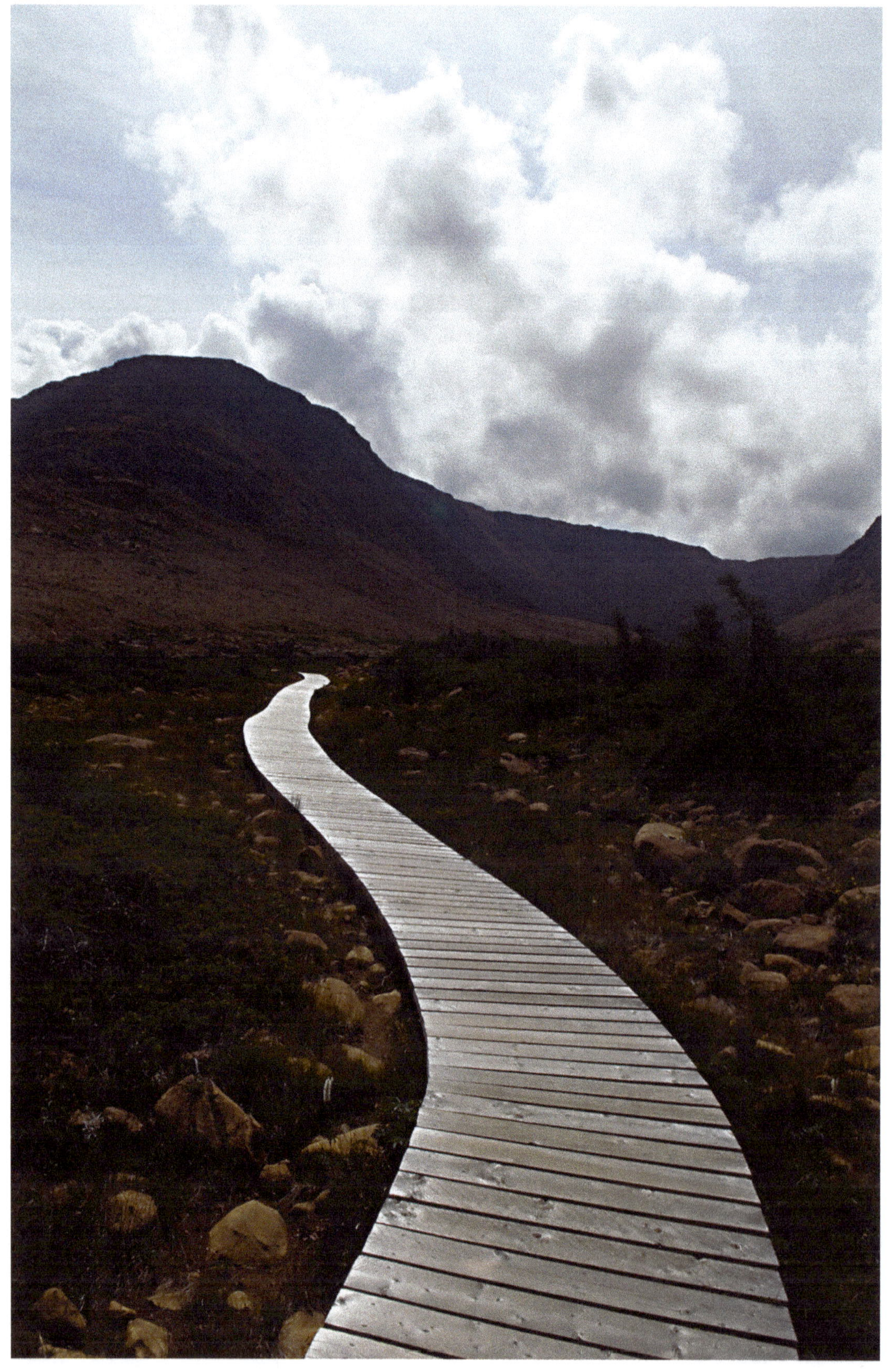

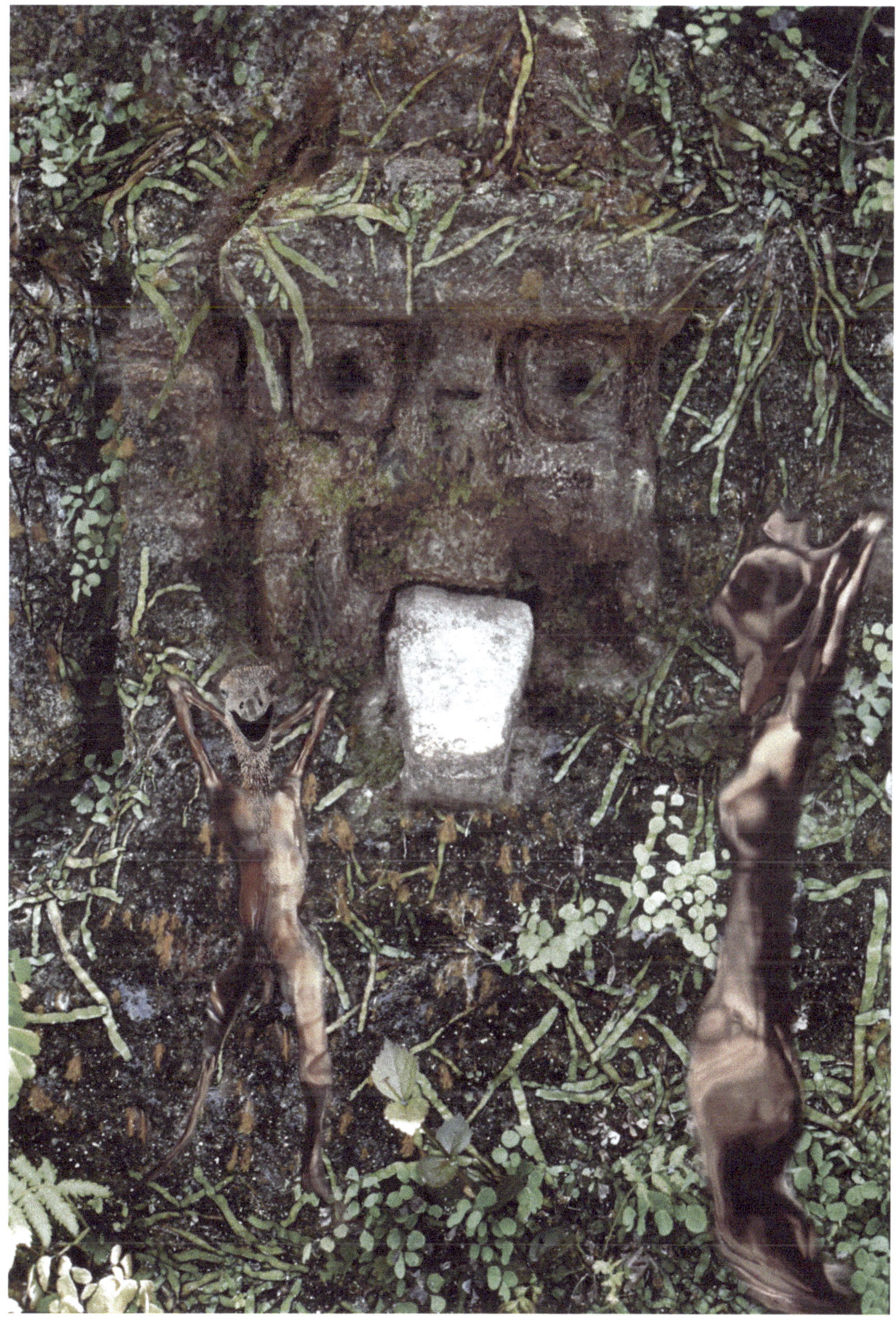

I sank into deep sleep and found myself at a pagan ritual, only parts of which I can relate. No words were spoken, but the participants seemed to be keeping time to the mantra in my head. It was the chorus to an old Kingston Trio song. “Back to back. Belly to belly. Don’t give a damn cause I done that already. Back to back. Belly to belly at the zombie jamboree.” I was hoping for some sort of sexual encounter, but the scene took on a religious tone and I began looking for a way to excuse myself without attracting attention.

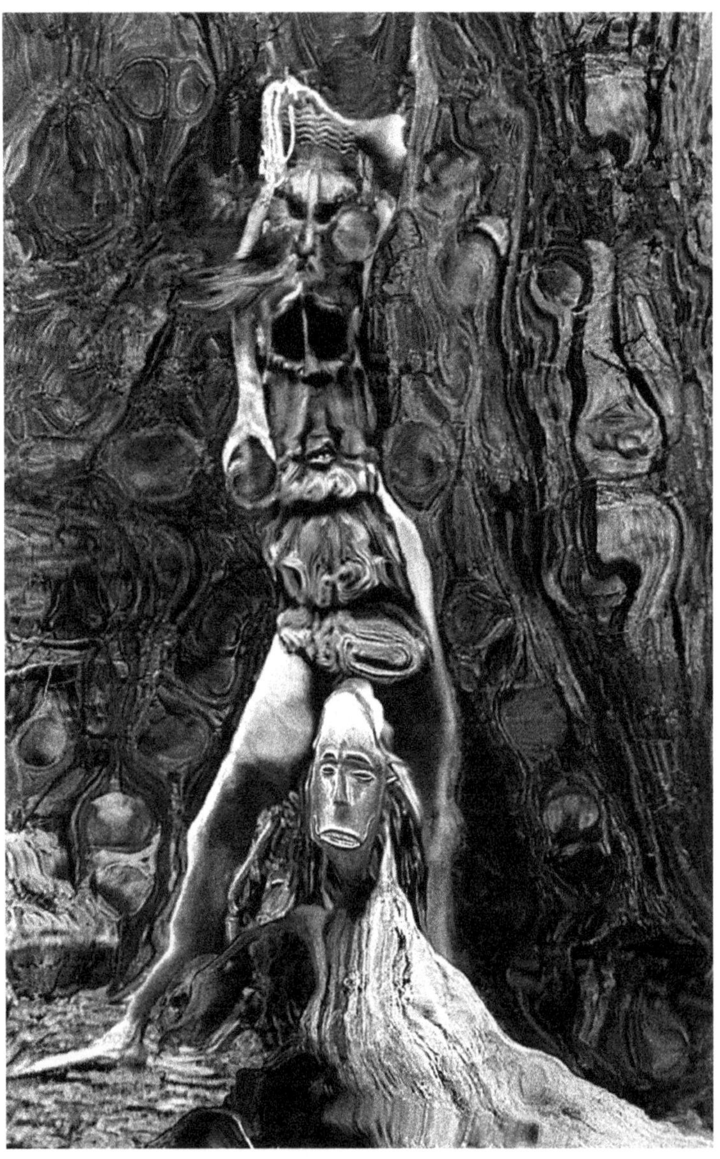

One of the best things about dream world is the ability to control events. As I mentioned earlier, lucid dreamers can bend situations to suit their desires. My skills have progressed to the point where I can dream hop. The result is similar to changing television channels without a guide, or jumping from the lion’s den into a snake pit. I go someplace else, but there is no preview.

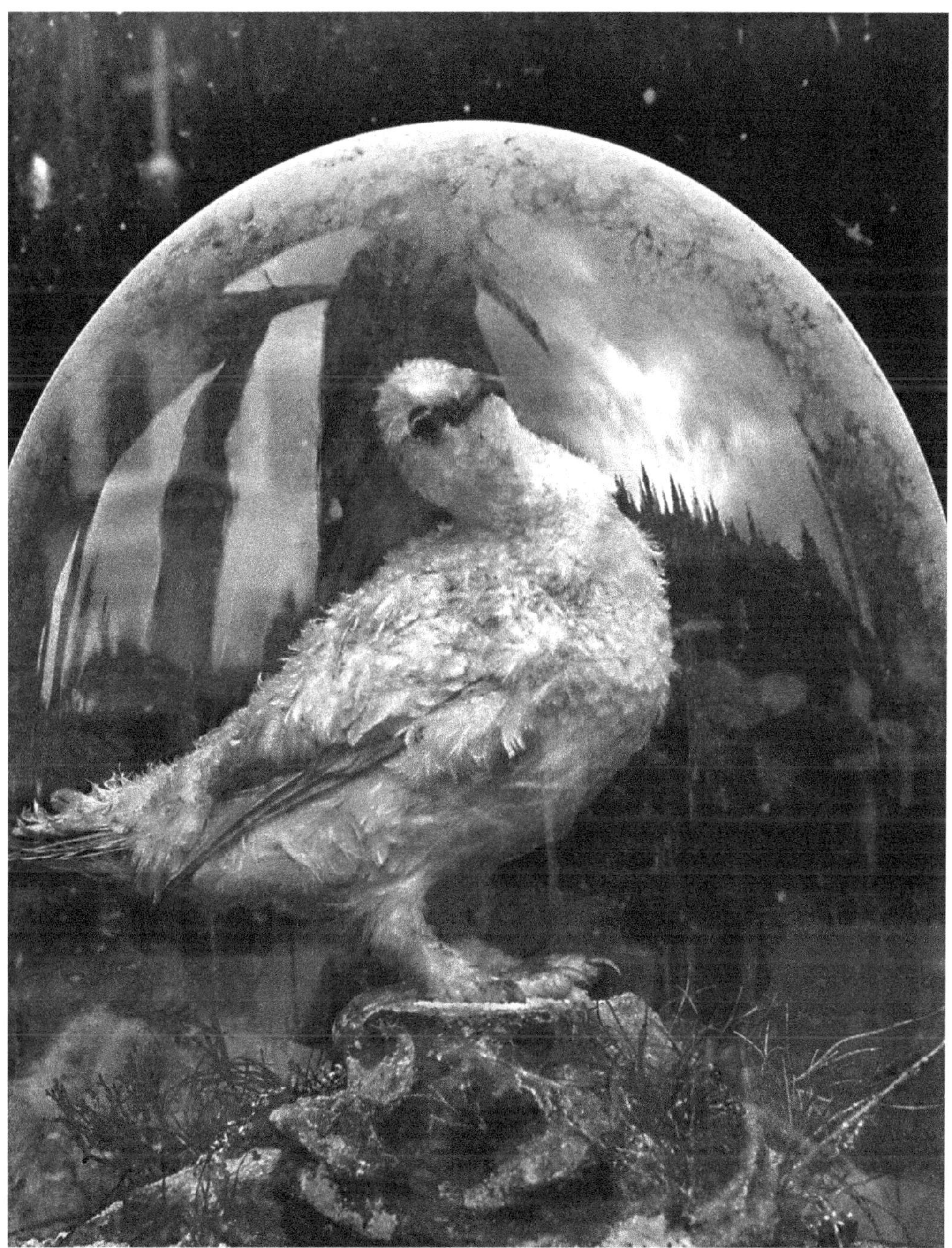

That is how I came to be looking at this chicken under glass from my perch behind the tree. It was a reasonable dream, and I would have stayed there if I had not become a monkey in a somewhat compromising situation.

So I made another exit, and became a horse skull, a friend of the angel that was heralding another Texas heat wave. It was hot enough to melt a dog, and I began to wish I could go back to being a monkey.

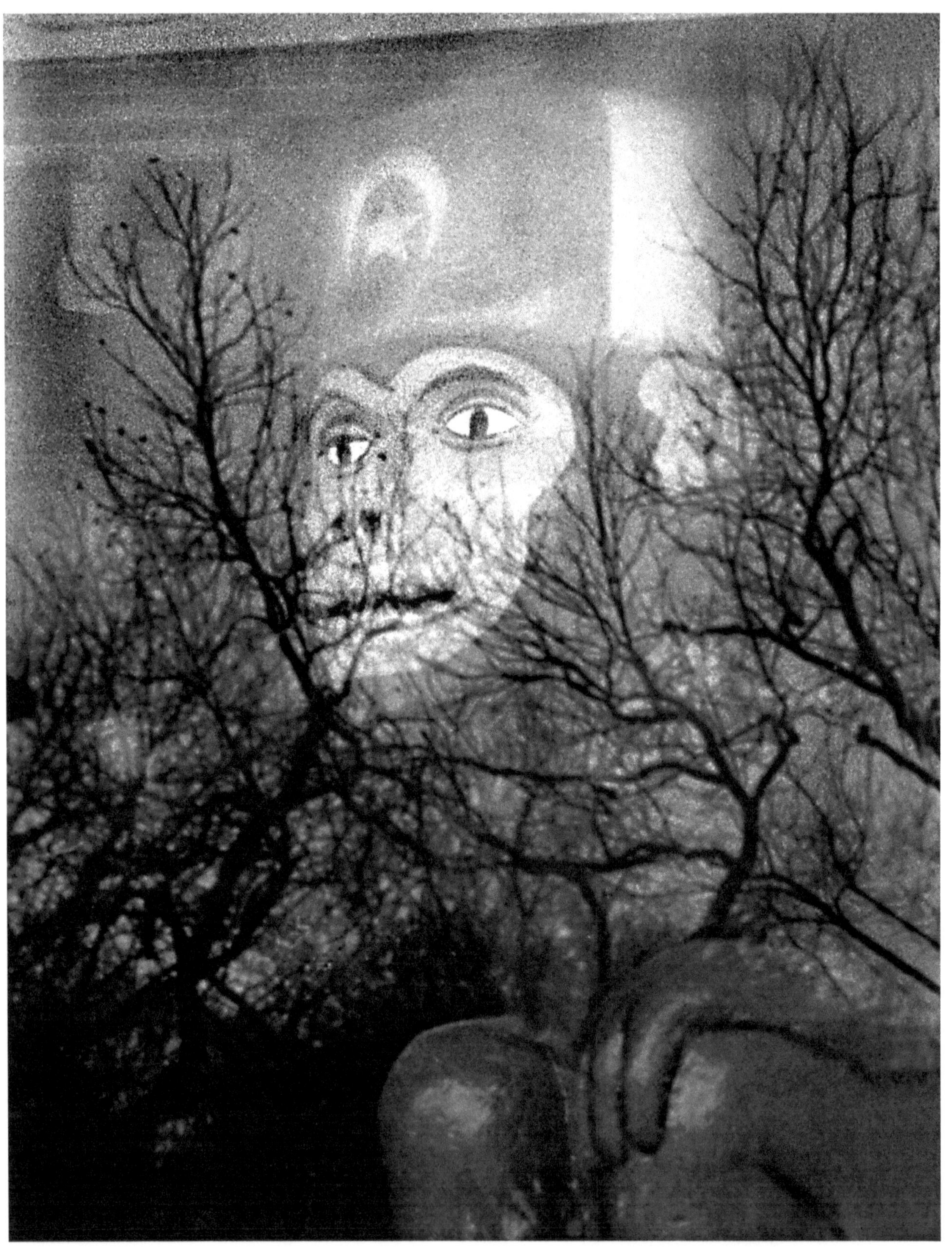

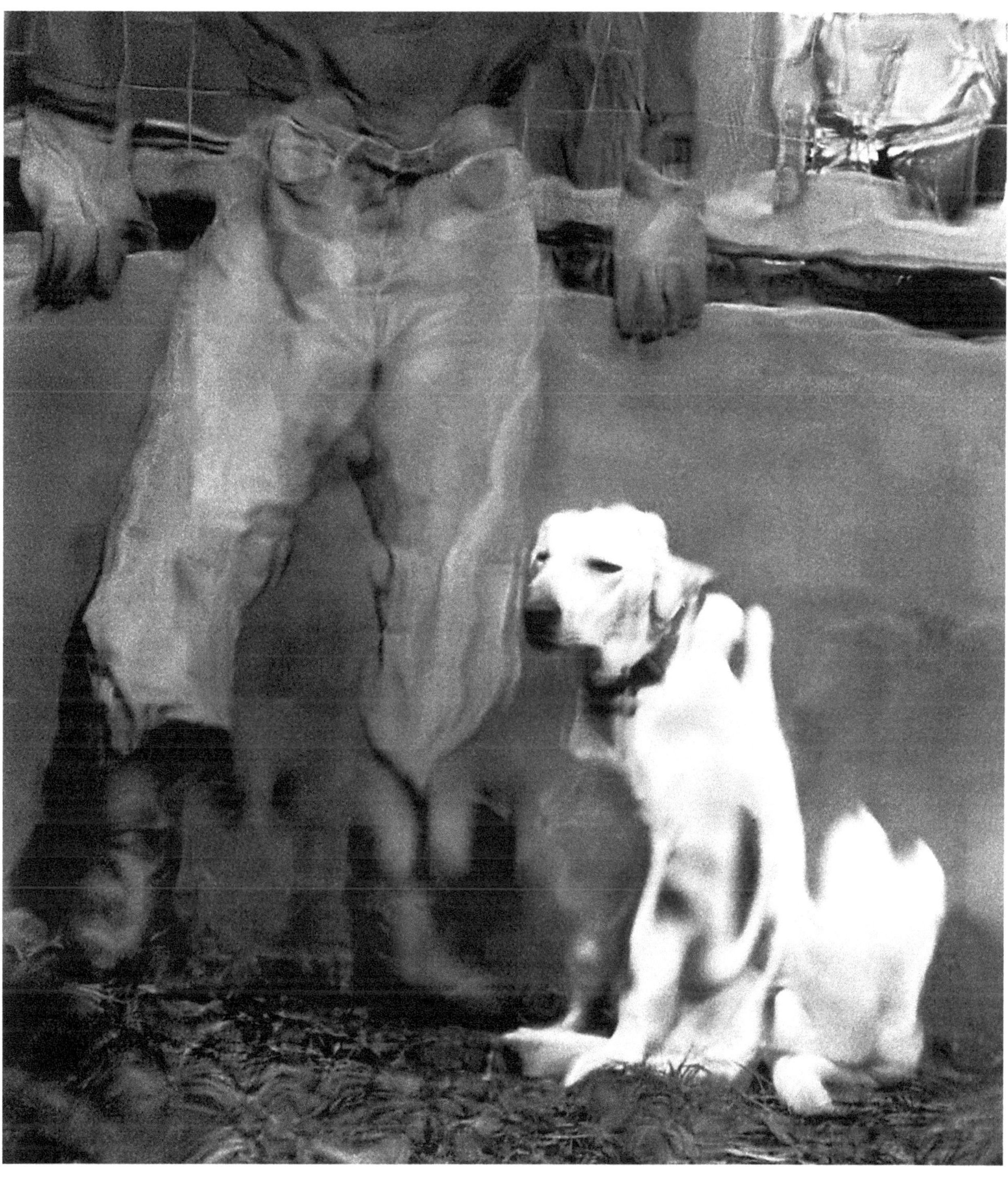

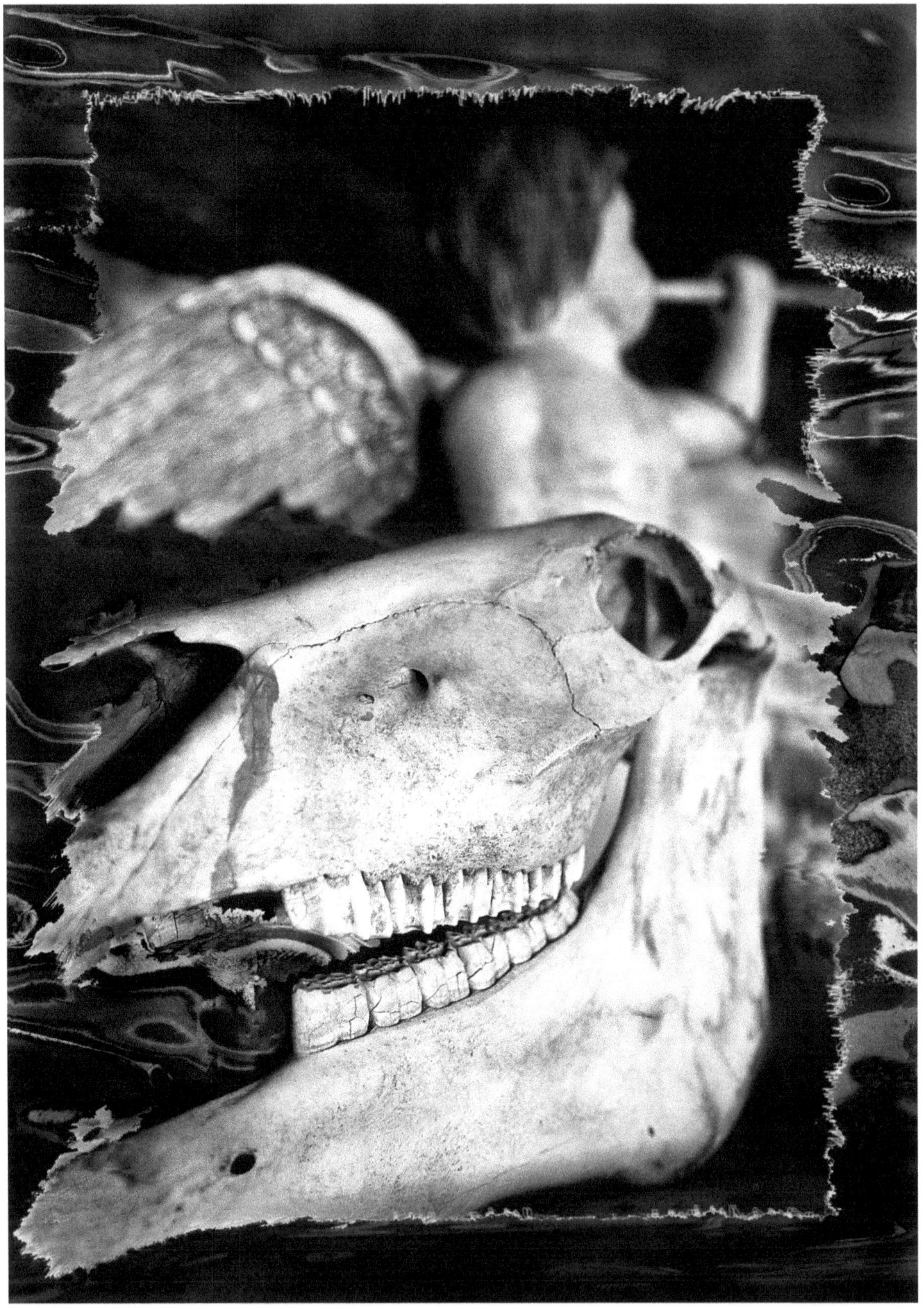

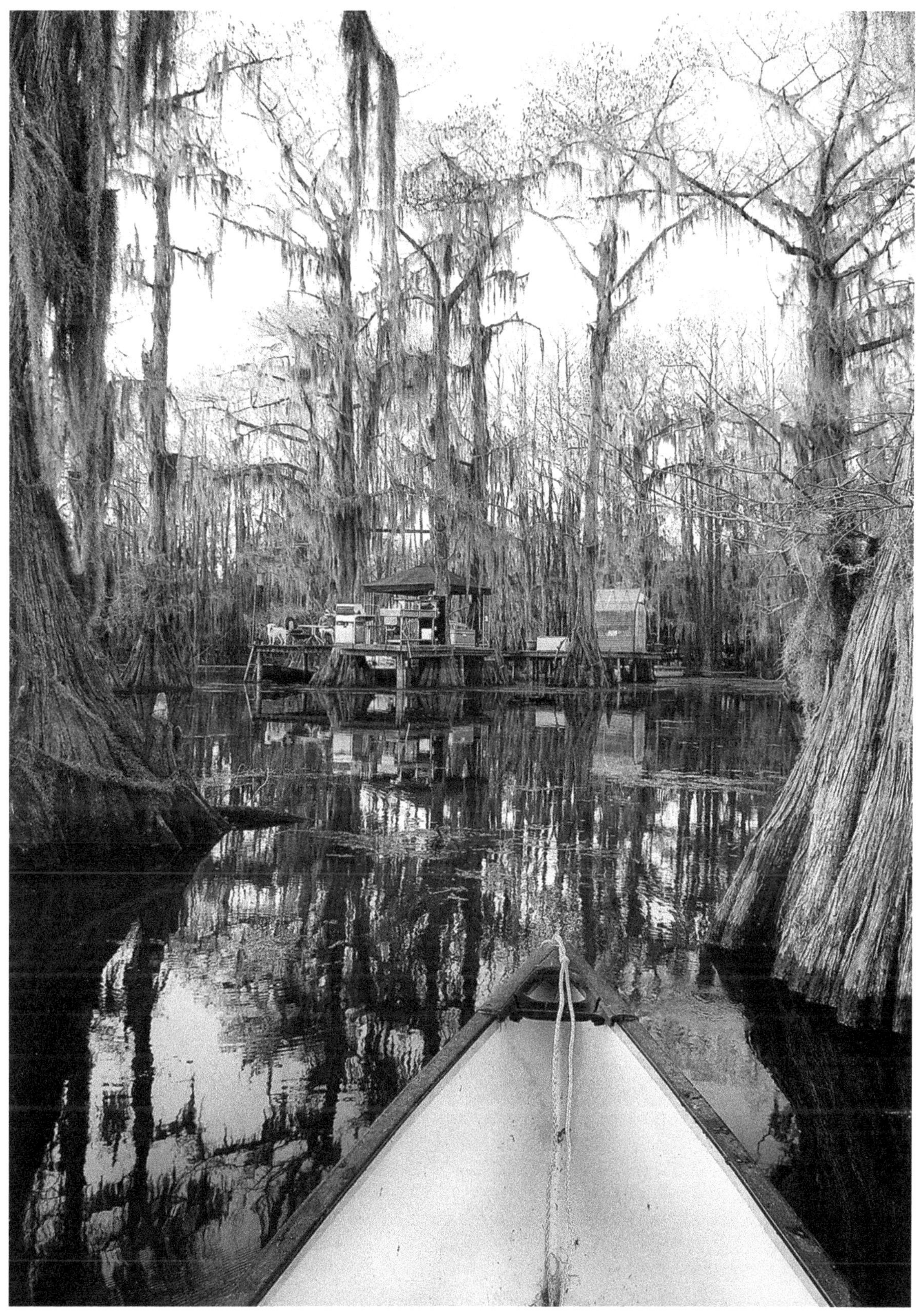

There is a place I have been to with my wife and dog that can be reached from almost all directions by water. It is a rental cabin with a pier and several small boats and canoes. Sometimes I visit a similar location in my dreams and watch it morph into something unrecognizable. No matter how bizarre the dream becomes, the feeling is of familiarity and comfort, and I have no desire to change course.

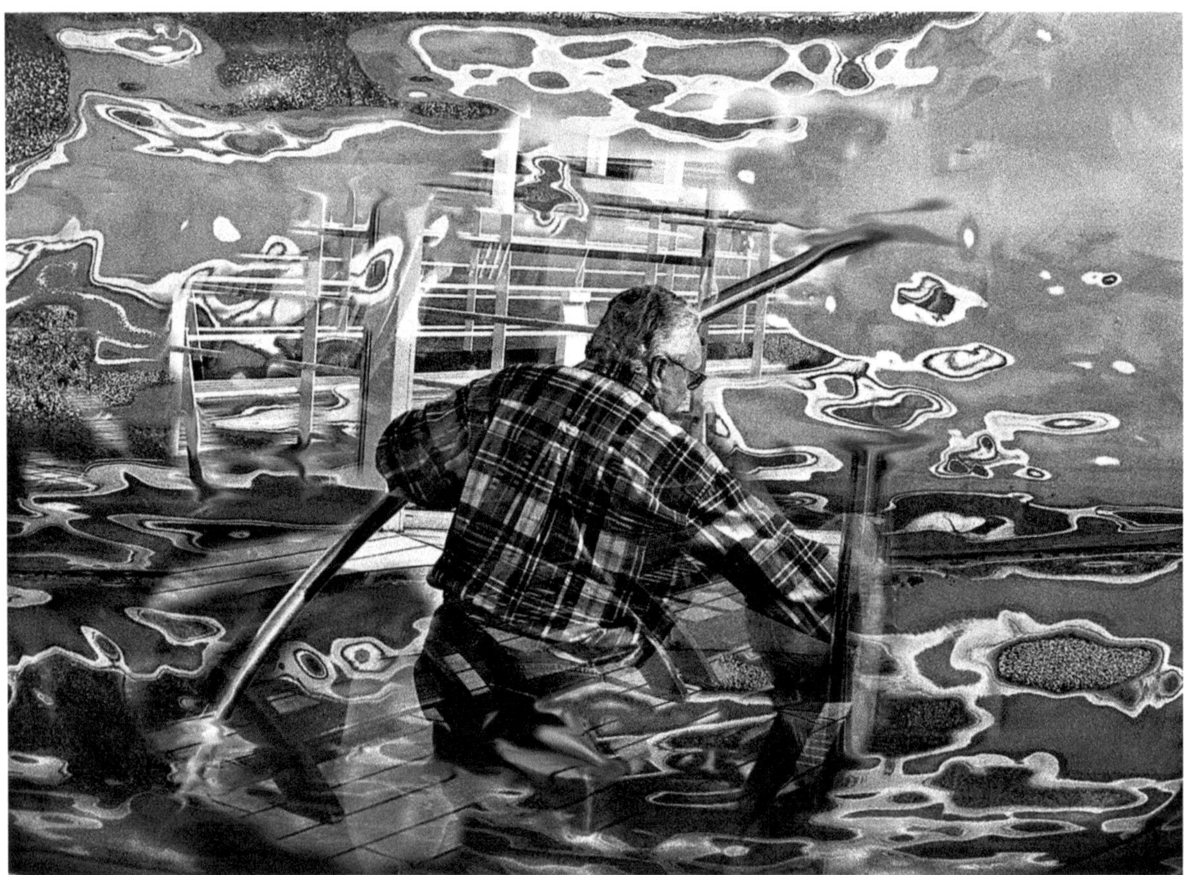

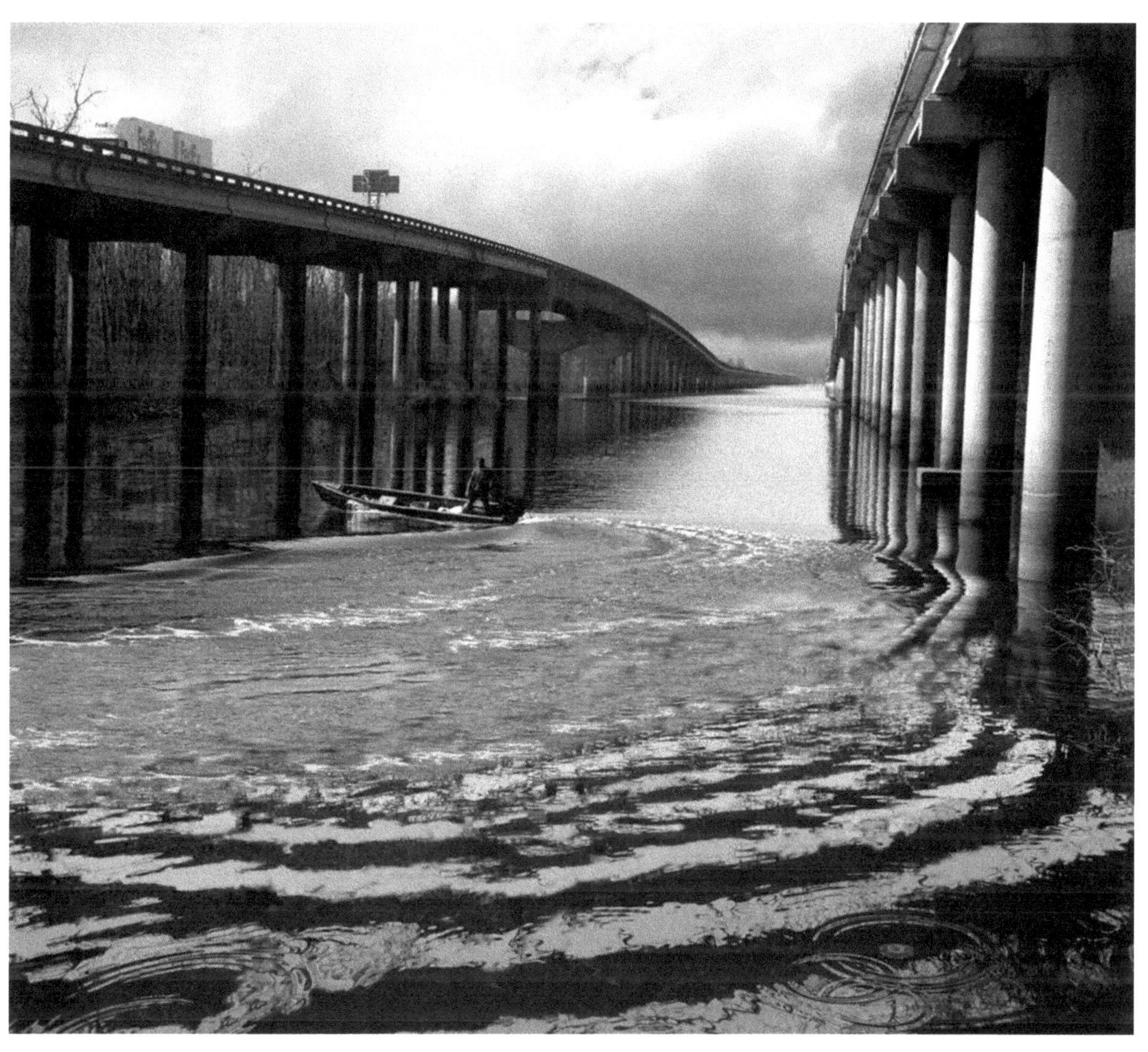

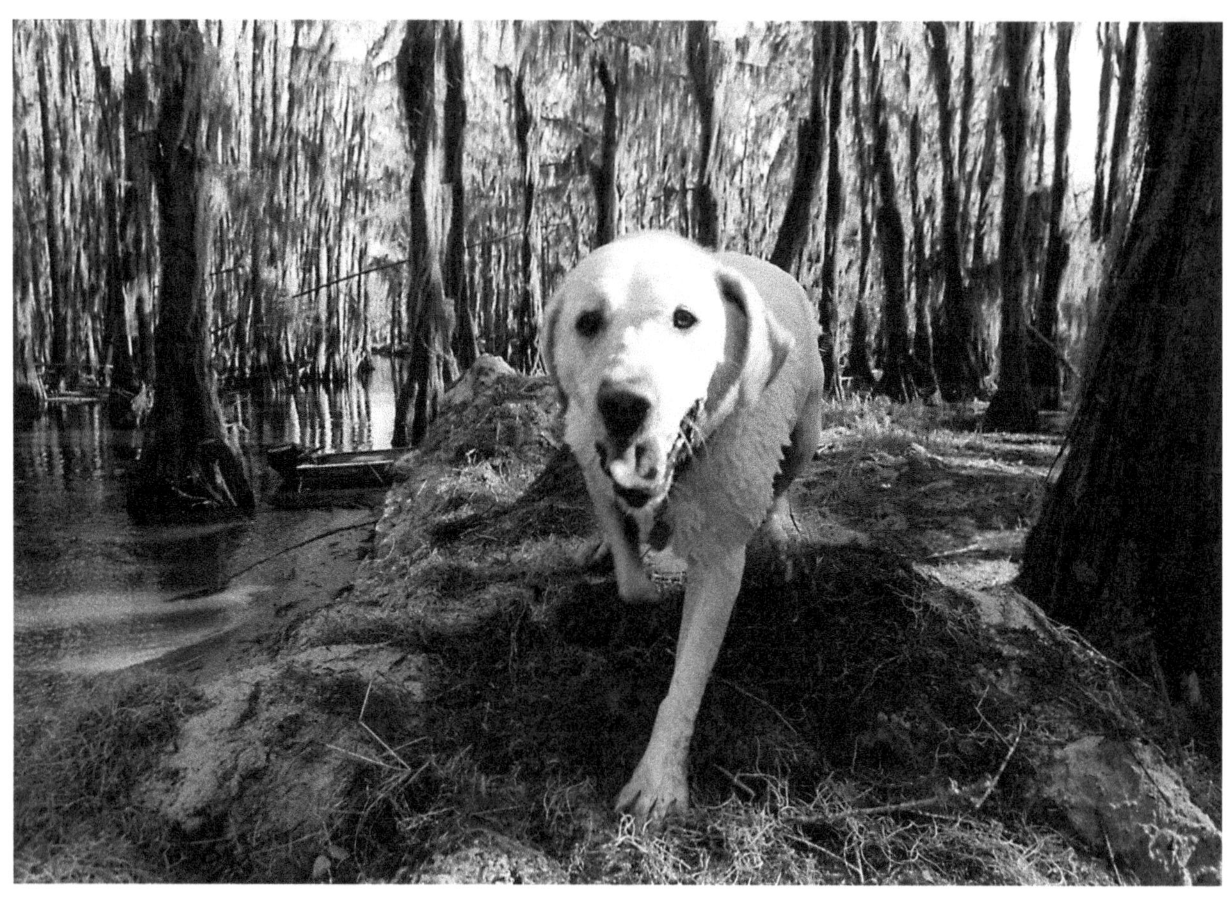

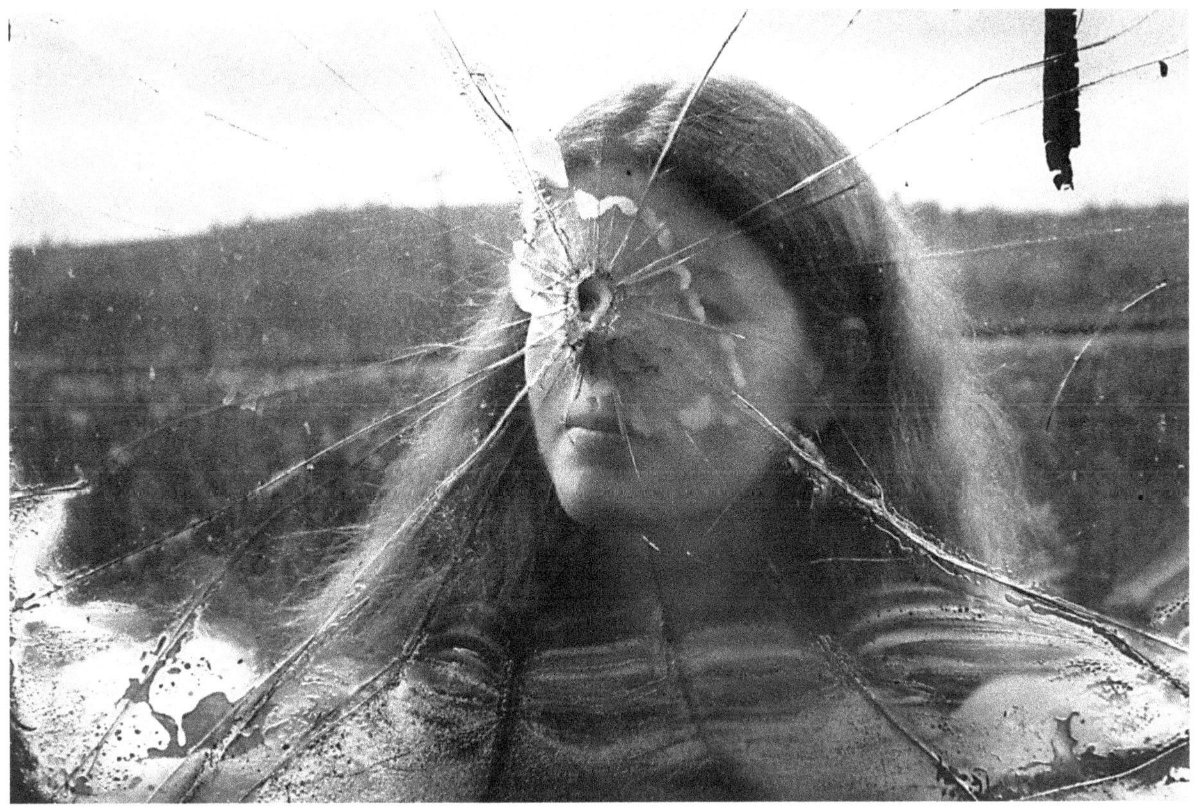

Does your mind tend to wander in the middle of the night? Does it play with your emotions? Mix lust and joy with fright? Does it view your life through a fictional lens? And take you to places your body has never been?

Familiar and strange visions and feelings. They make dreams confusing, and appealing. Dreams are ephemeral, and elusive. They get into your head. They're intrusive.

And when you catch one, what have you got? Did it happen in real life? Probably not. It's just something your subconscious decided to show. "This was lodged in your brain. Thought you should know."

Hard to remember, and easy to dismiss. Dreams are what they are. Whatever that is.

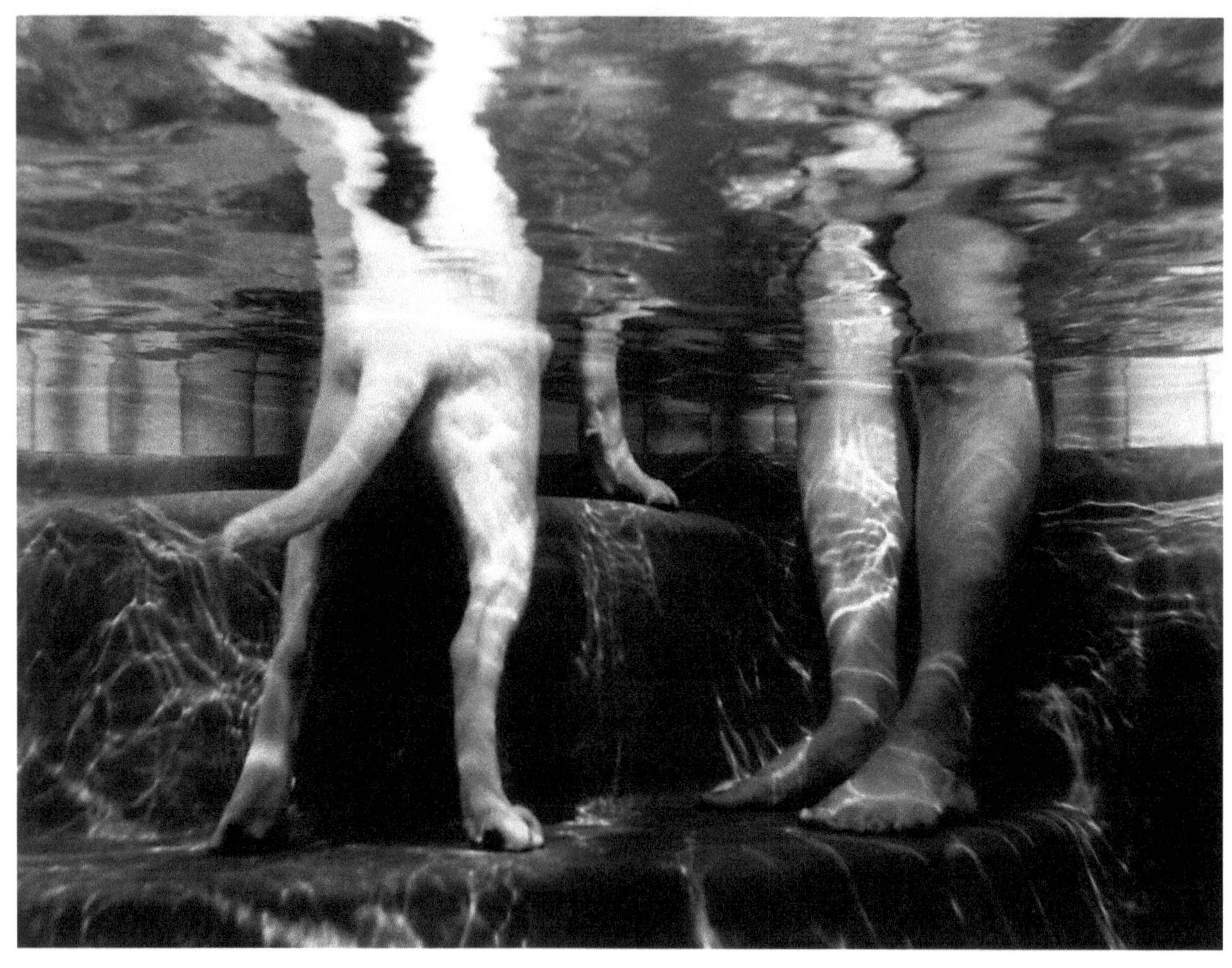

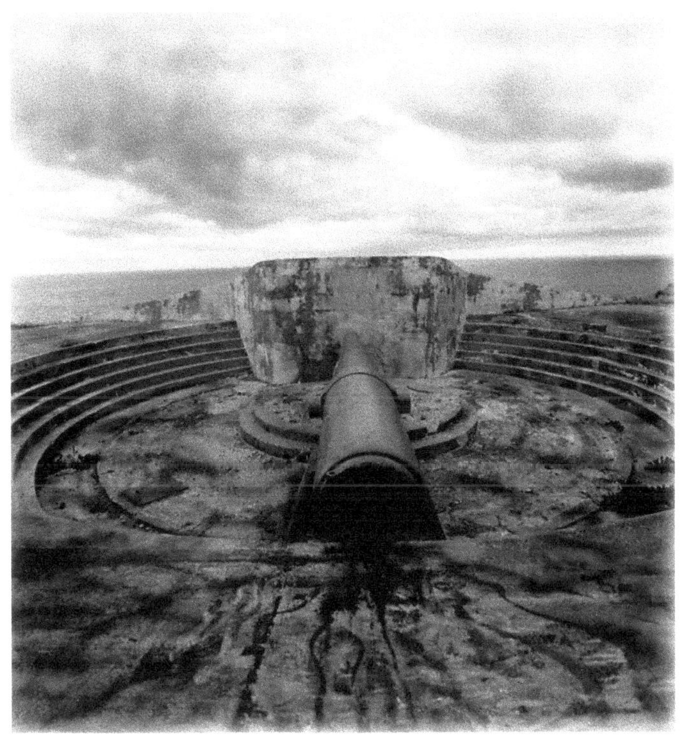

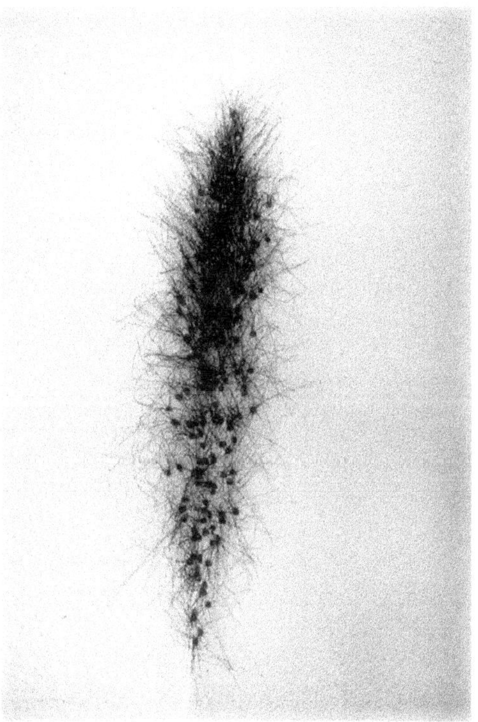

Once, I dreamed I was the judge at an obscenity trial and it was my duty to decide whether certain shapes and forms were vulgar.

The objects were round or bulbous, and very smooth. I had to admit they were seductive, especially the way they were displayed.

Everything was white. The exhibits and the pedestals they were on, the floor and ceiling were painted white, and bathed in light that reflected from every direction, so there were no shadows. There were at least a dozen shapes, each one supported by a pedestal that was every bit as sensual and probably more phallic than the objects I was to pass judgment on.

I don't remember thinking about the lack of straight lines or hard angles, but I did consider the overall scene to be tipped in the direction of censorship.

Nothing was outright vulgar, but some of the pieces were provocative. The idea of passing judgment on inanimate shapes and forms was troubling, and the weight of my responsibility was so disturbing that I worried myself awake.

The reason I have dreams like this could be that I look for such things to photograph in waking life. Nature and the man-made environment, and even those places where the two interact, are full of variety, by accident and by design. The photograph of daddy longlegs spiders in a corner is the closest example I could find of vulgar design, and that may be mostly because of the way I feel about spiders.

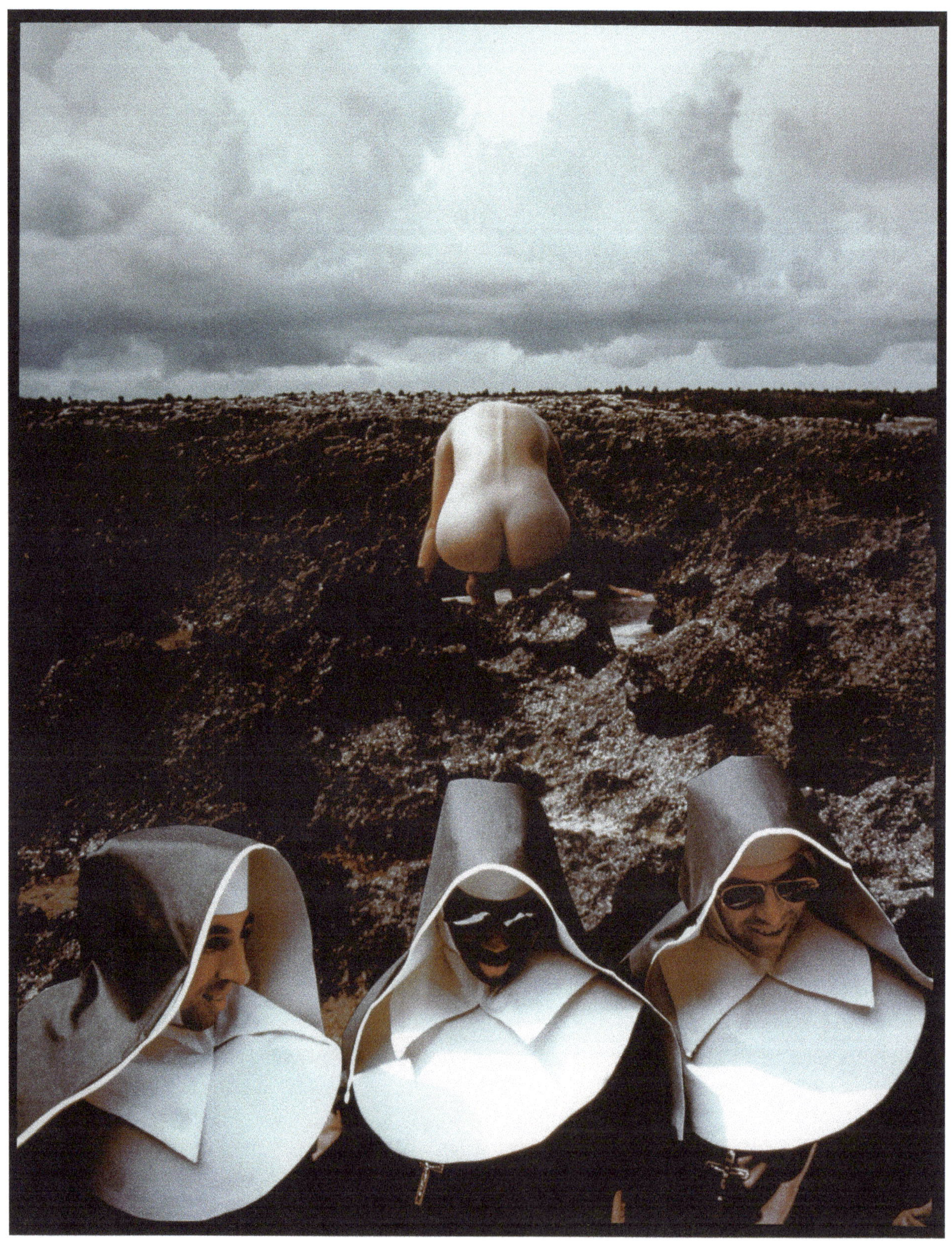

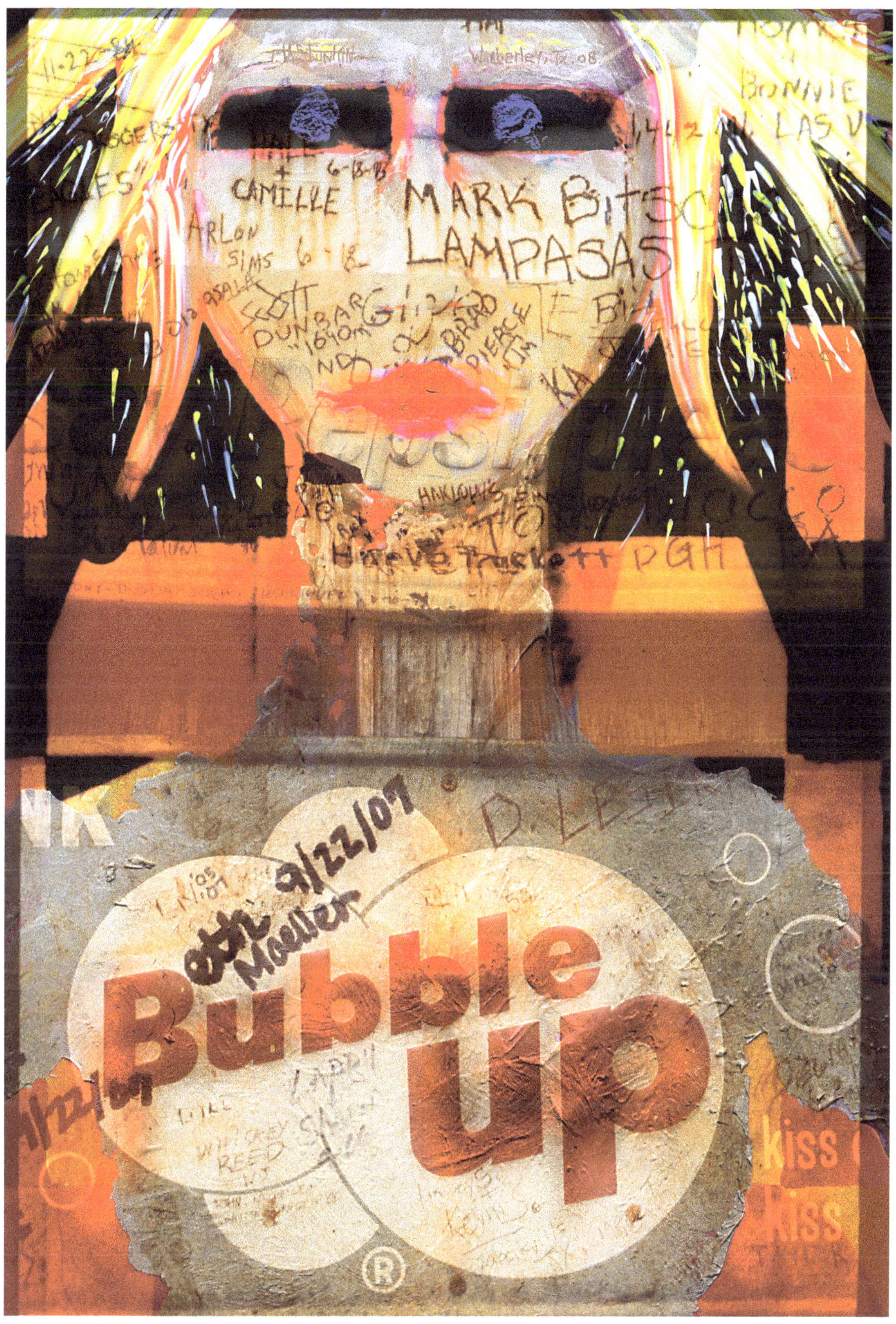
CAMILLE
MARK BITS
LAMPASAS
ARLON
SIMS
9/22/09
Bubble
up
kiss
Kiss

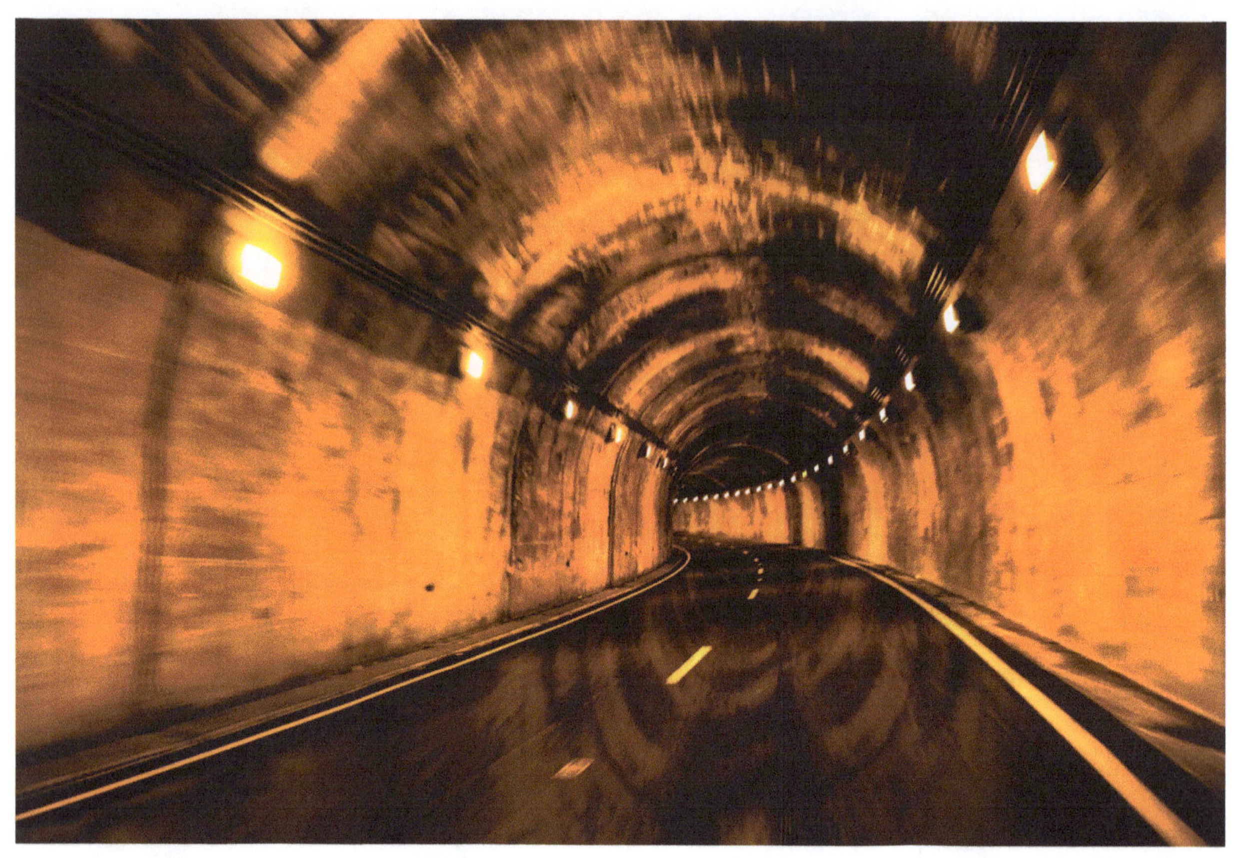

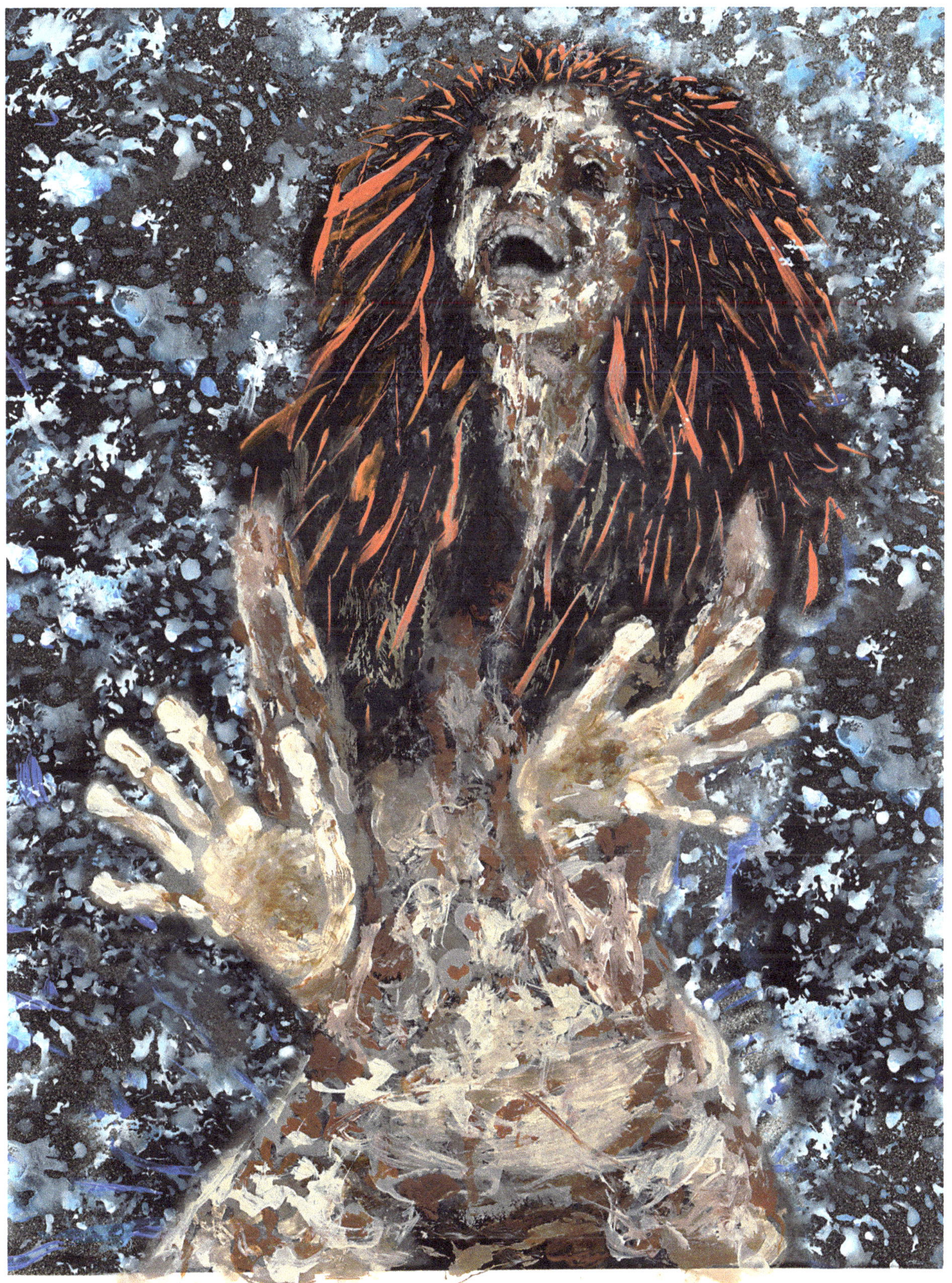

When allowed to drift, the mind seems to labor over what may be important, so dreams often mirror lifetime obsessions.

Sex is a fixation that elicits a large amount of brain wave activity. A University of Montreal study has found that about eight percent of men's and women's dreams were of an erotic nature. The amount seems conservative when you consider the fact that dream sex feels almost as good as the real thing, but is about 100 percent safer.

On the other hand, when your sleeping mind has you coupling with people and things your daytime thoughts consider taboo, dream sex can be uncomfortable. Social conditioning may compel us to mix a little guilt with our pleasure.

For whatever reason, our desires often become enmeshed in a web of insecurity and fear. Some analysts have concluded that dreams about being naked in public may reflect feelings of shame or vulnerability.

As a pubescent boy there was no way I could go to sleep and not dream about sex. Even when I did not remember my dreams, I knew what they had been about. Until I read in the Boy Scouts Handbook about nocturnal emissions, I thought I had a problem that was too embarrassing to talk about. "It's Okay," the book informed me. I was healthy and normal, and somewhere between being a boy and a man. St. Augustine, the pious priest who coined the phrase "original sin" forgave himself for his nocturnal misdeeds, so why couldn't I do the same?

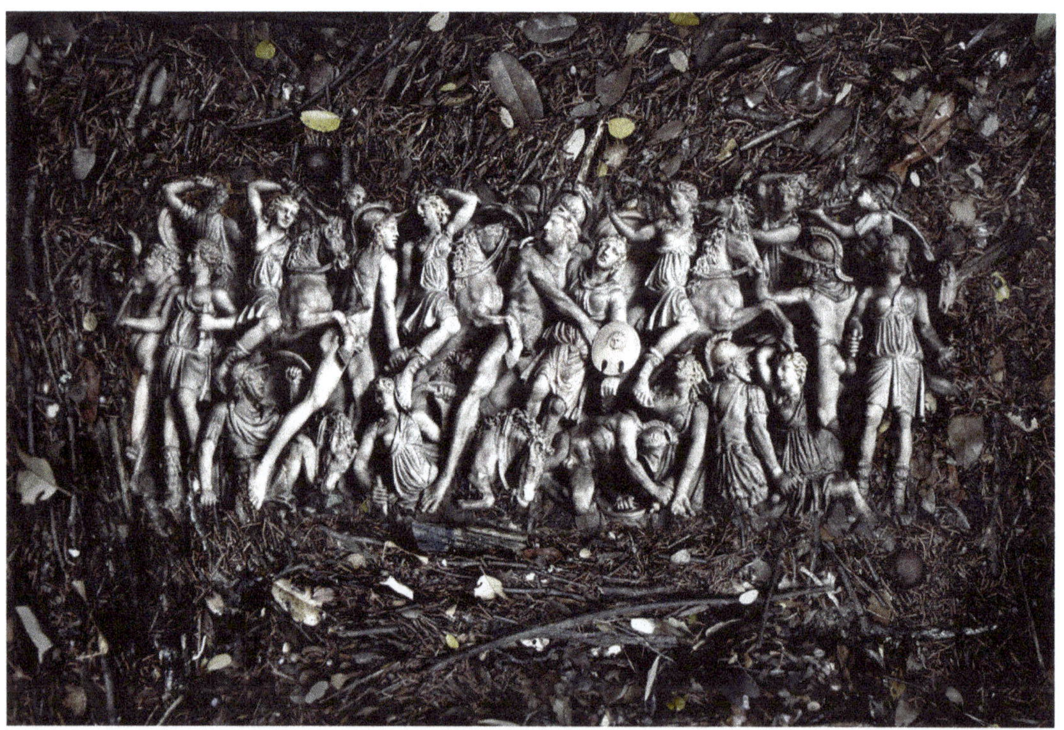

Sigmund Freud reasoned that most dreams represent some form of sexual repression. Compare some sexual dream theories with your own dreams and you quickly realize either just how messed up you really are or that not all dream theories apply.

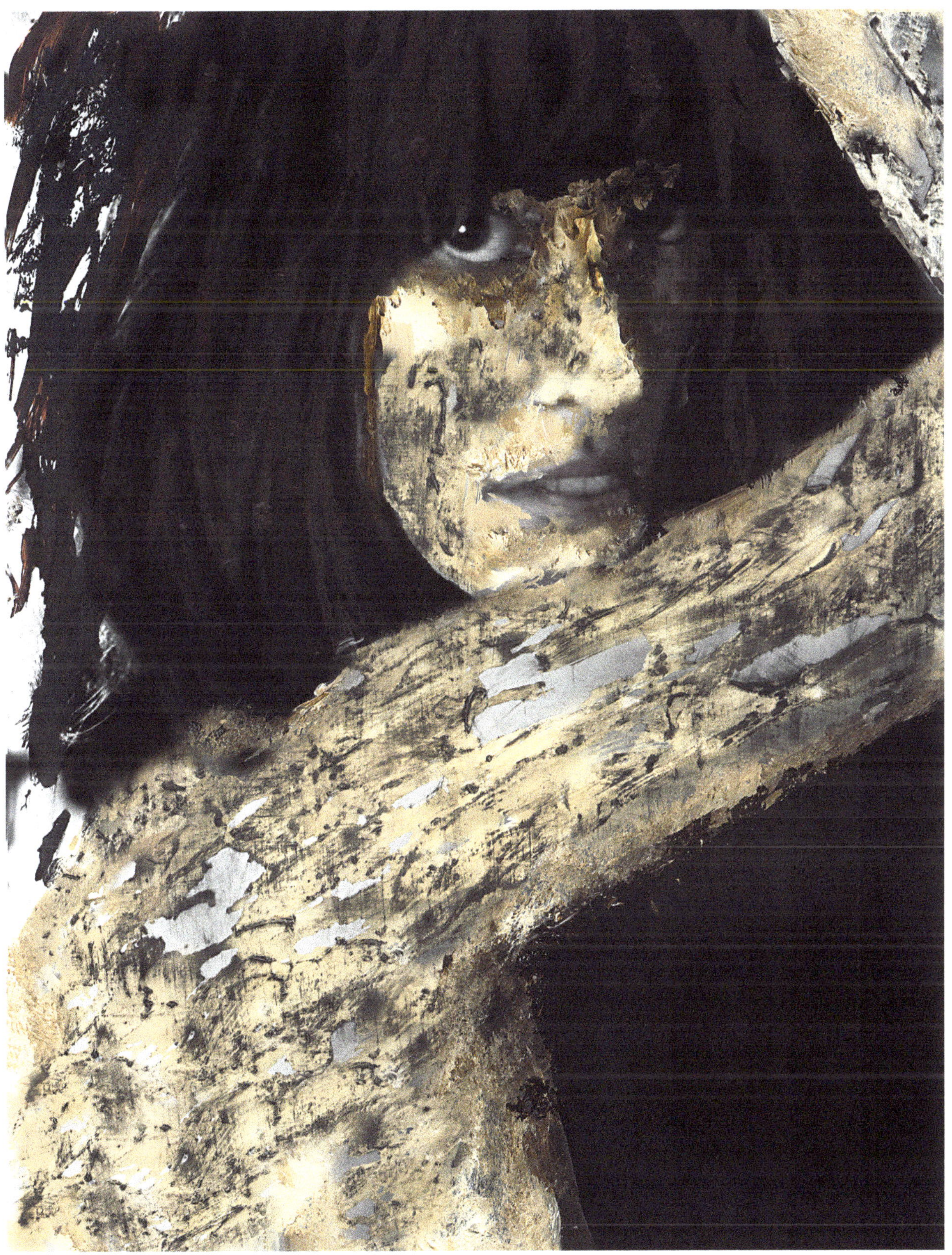

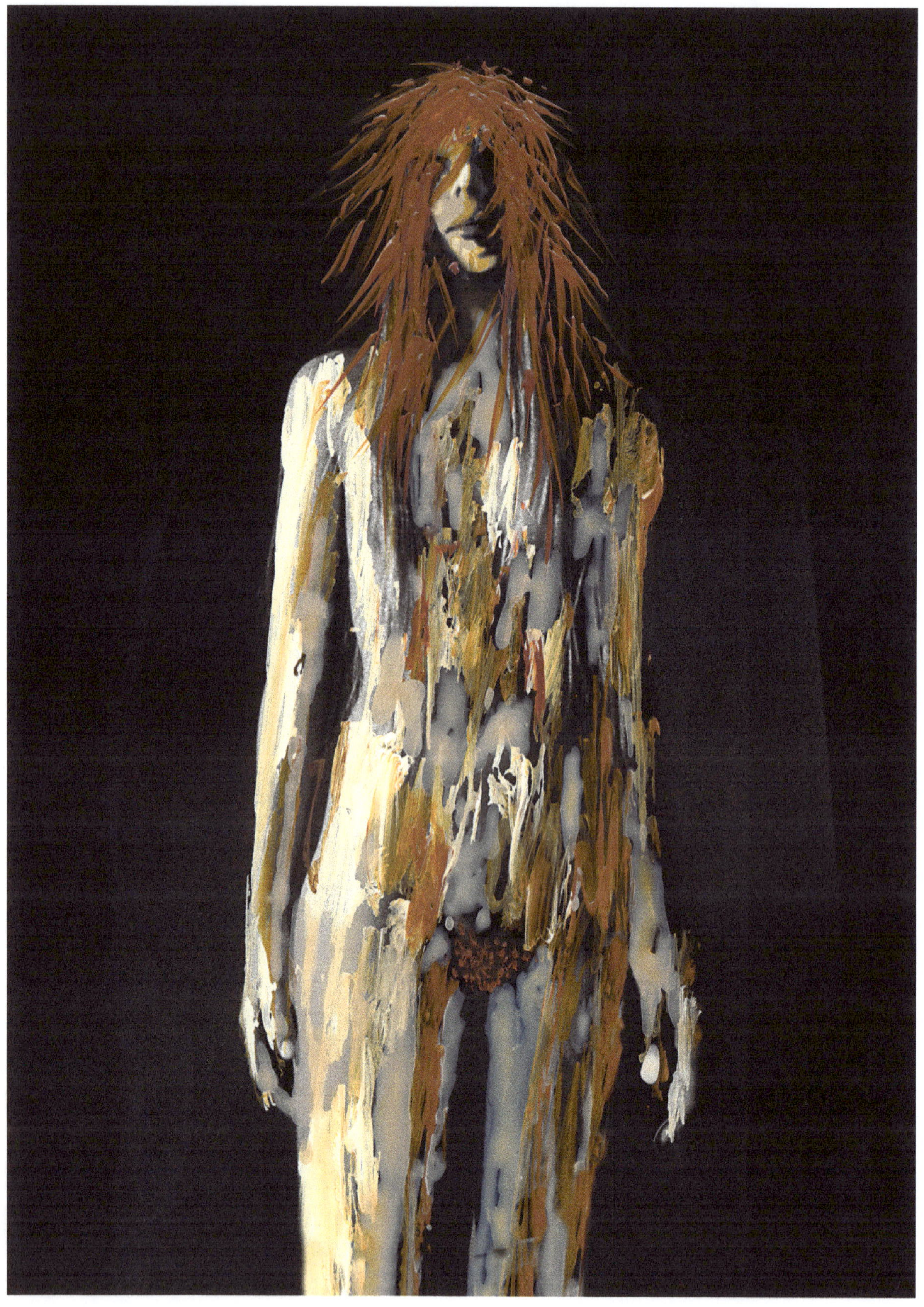

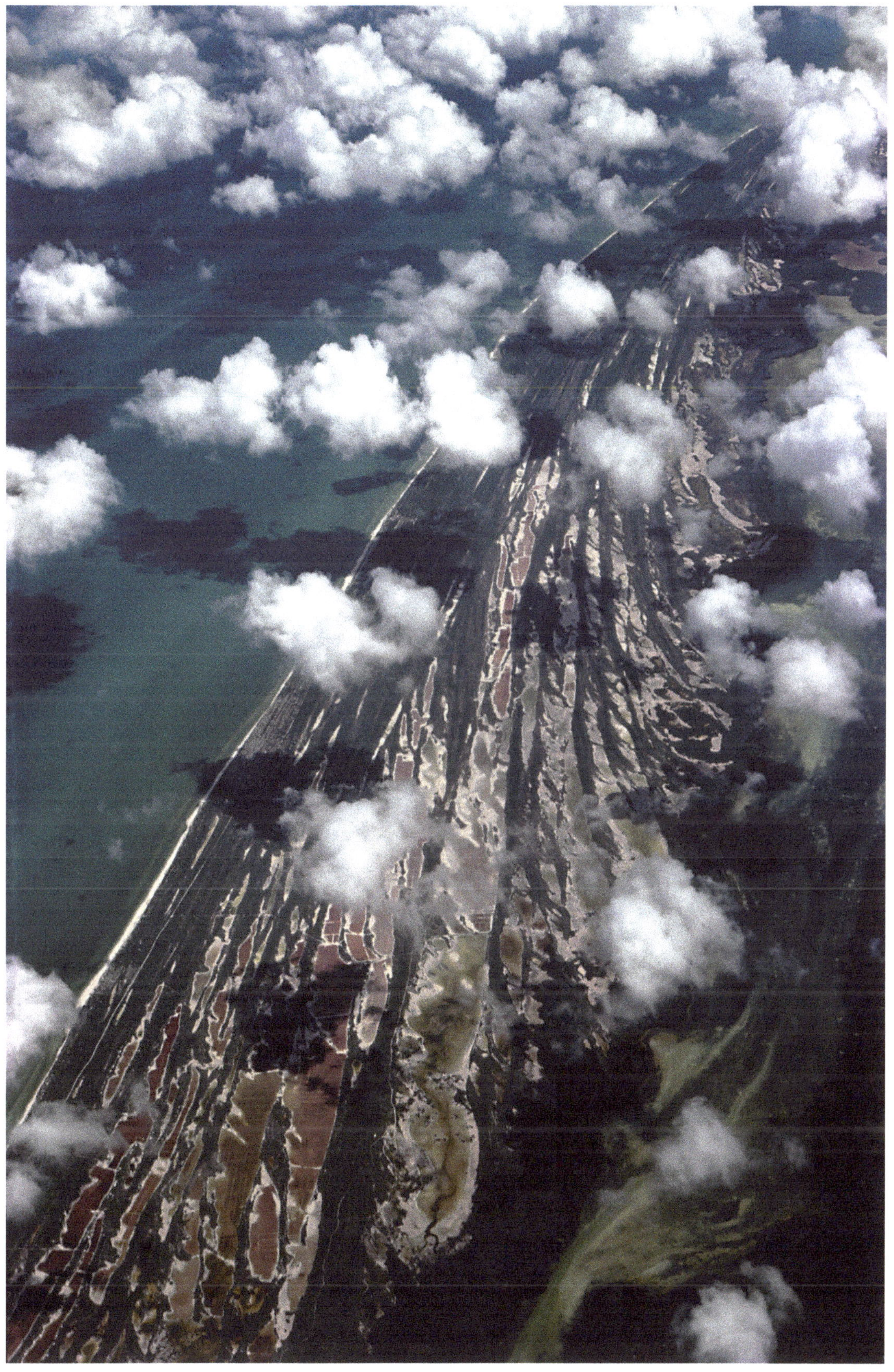

My Dad had a recurring dream about falling. It began in his childhood and reappeared at least once every five or ten years until he was in his 80s.

He said the fact that he was plummeting through the clouds toward earth never bothered him because he knew he was going to land in a wagon full of cotton. So, he enjoyed that dream, which began before he ever saw an airplane and continued long after he became an Air Force pilot.

I had a very pleasant dream once that involved flying. It began with my holding onto a garden hose that slowly lifted me into the air. At first the hose was in control, moving me across the sky in long slow arcs. By the end of the dream I was still holding onto the hose, but the sensation was more like being held aloft by a balloon. I was able to control my flight by pointing the nozzle in various directions. It stretched so far that soon I was flying high over trees and houses. I flew over a lake and gently set down on the front porch of a house I did not know. My air travel ended there, and the dream morphed into another vision.

Some dream analysts relate flying dreams to liberation. Maybe so. For me, they hover in the realm of sweet dreams.

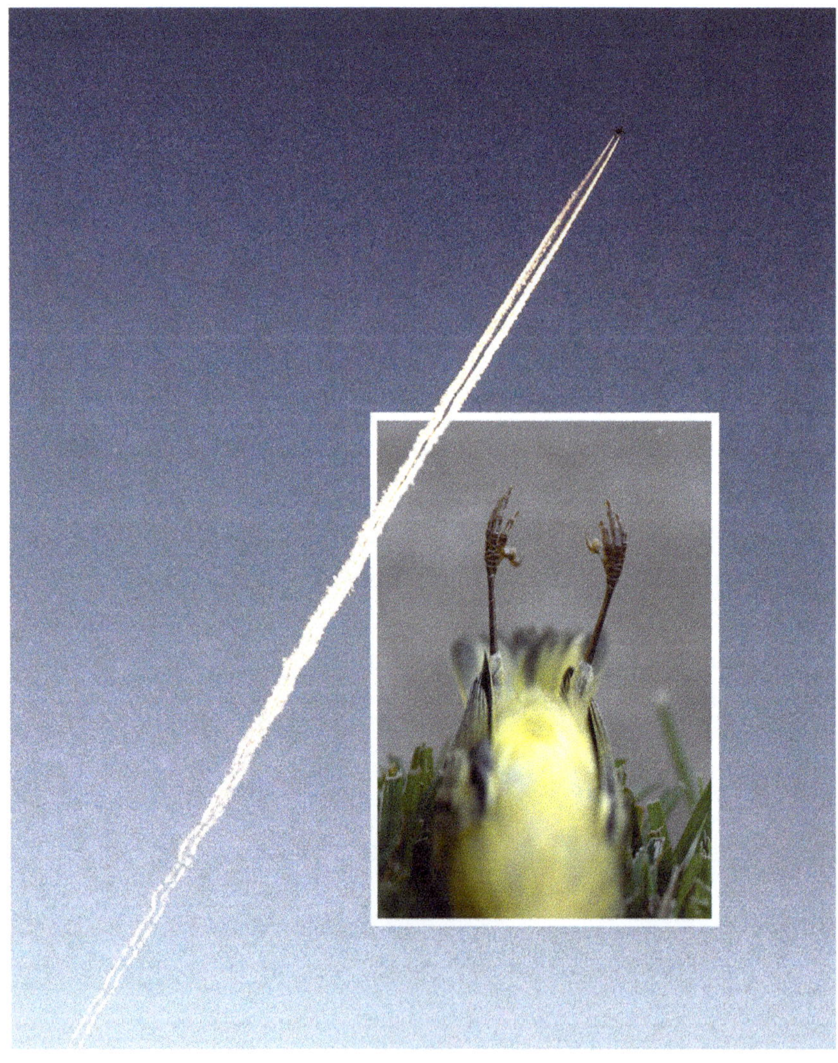

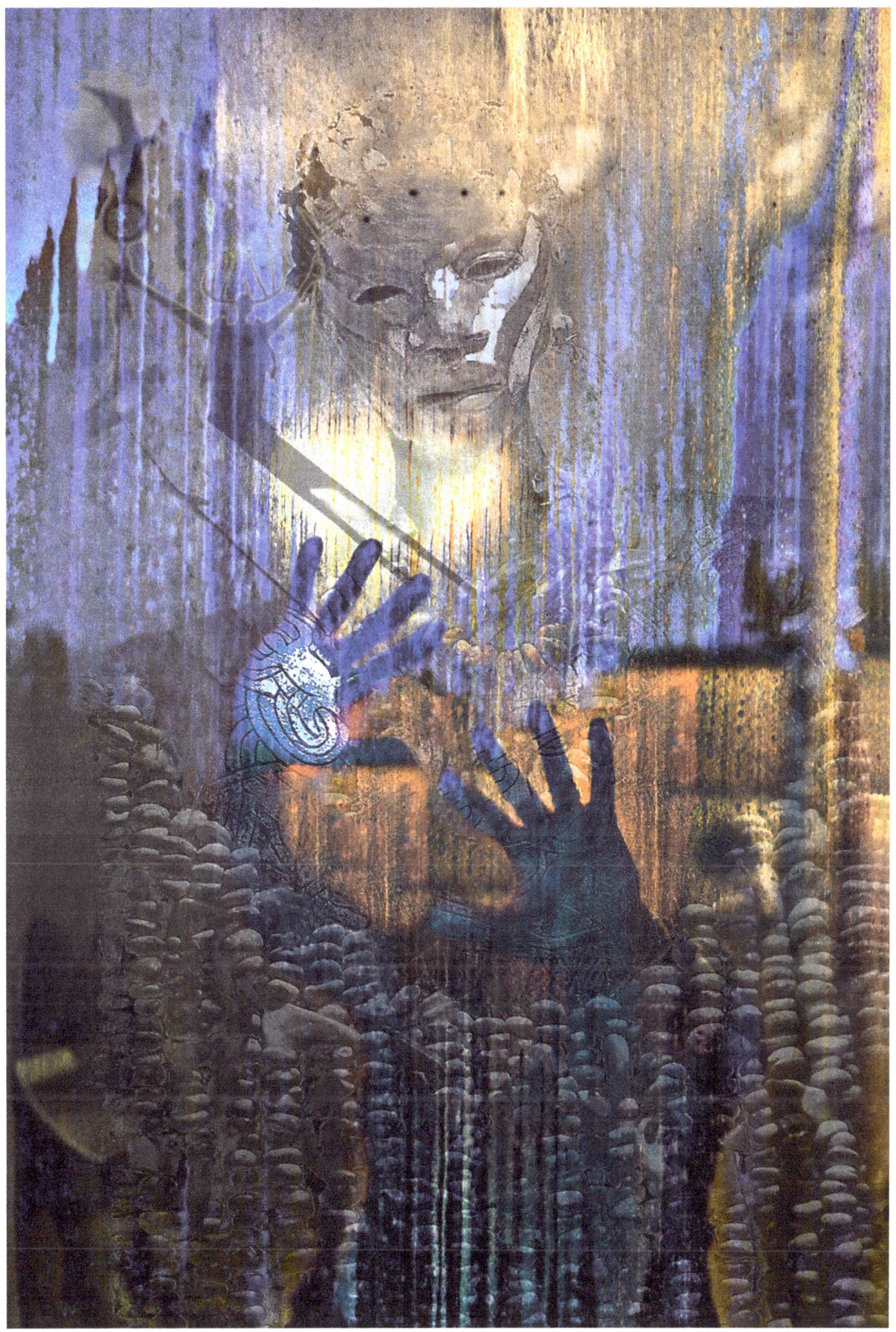

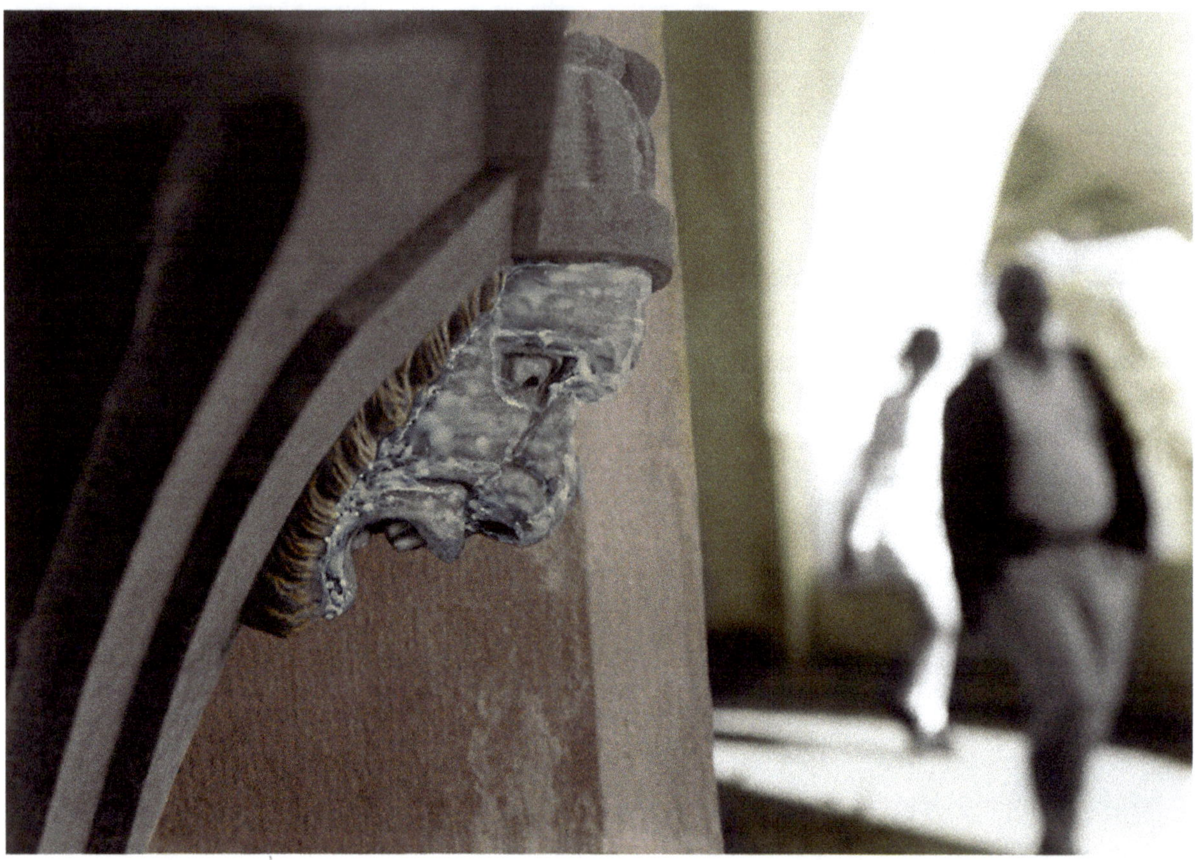

About 50,000 years ago, Homo sapiens and their newly developed cerebral cortexes invented shamans to interpret and possibly interact with the spirit world.

As that practice progressed, shamans employed ever-more inventive means of contacting the nether regions, and dream journeys became hallucinations or self-induced visions.

Since then, every major and at least one quasi-religion has harbored the belief that dreams offer a form of communication between the supernatural world and man.

Yet for practical purposes those same spiritual organizations remain skeptical of dream analysis in general. If everybody knew the path to the spirit world, the authority of organized religions would be diminished.

Nevertheless, religious dream references abound with about a hundred examples in the Old Testament and over two hundred in the Talmud. Joseph Smith received the Book of Mormon in a dream, and Mohammed's subconscious was the path of divine messages from God.

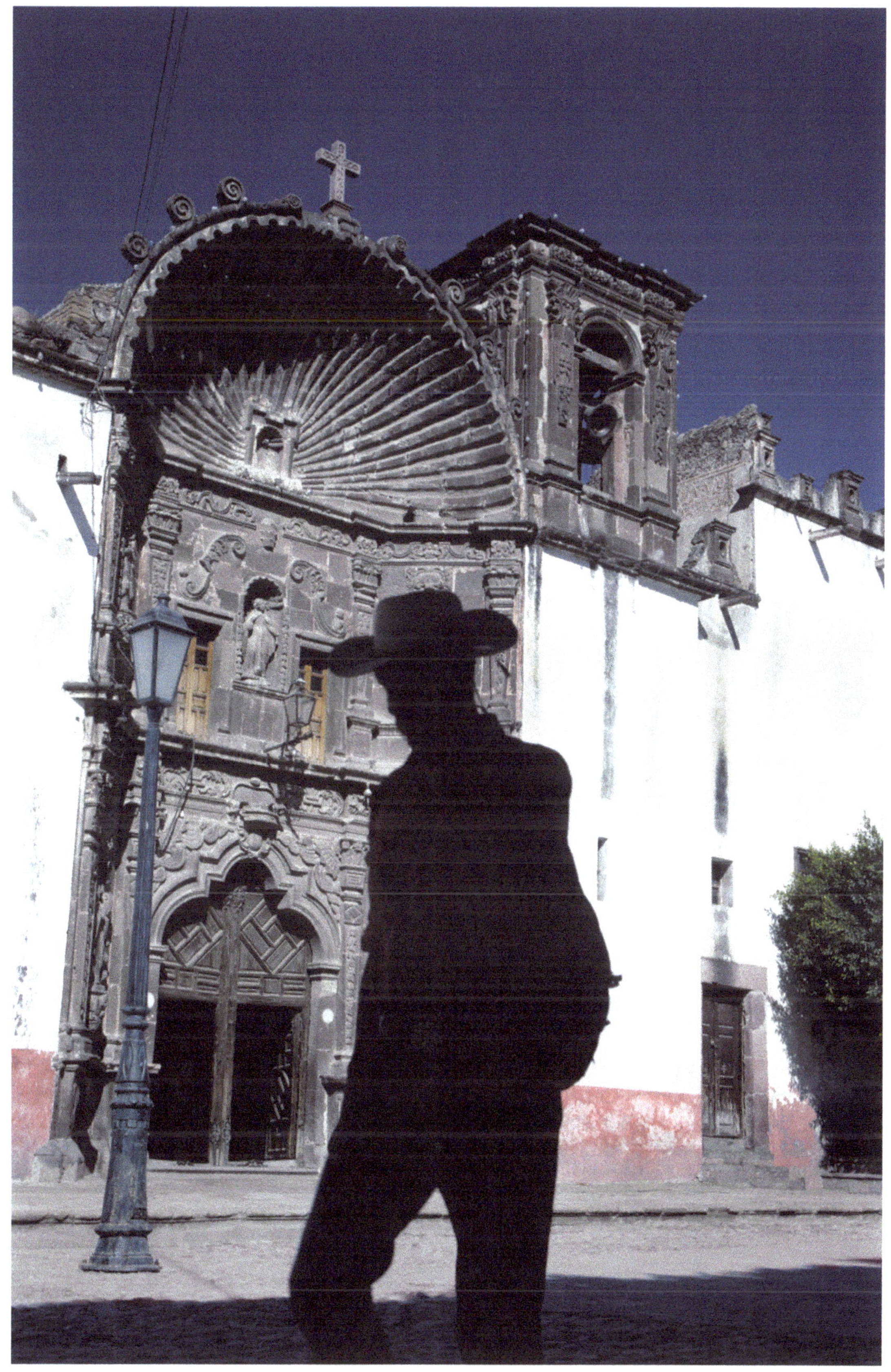

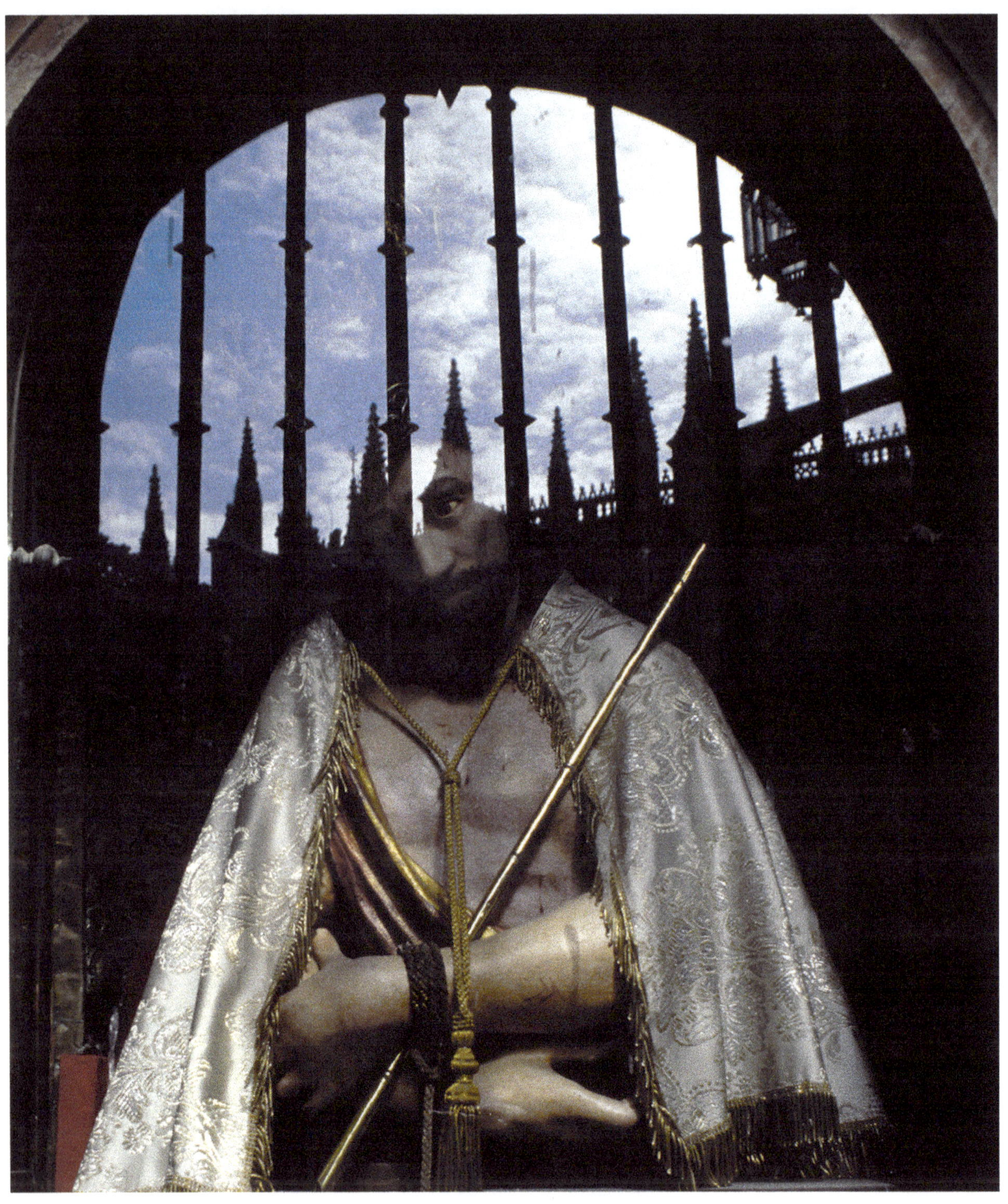

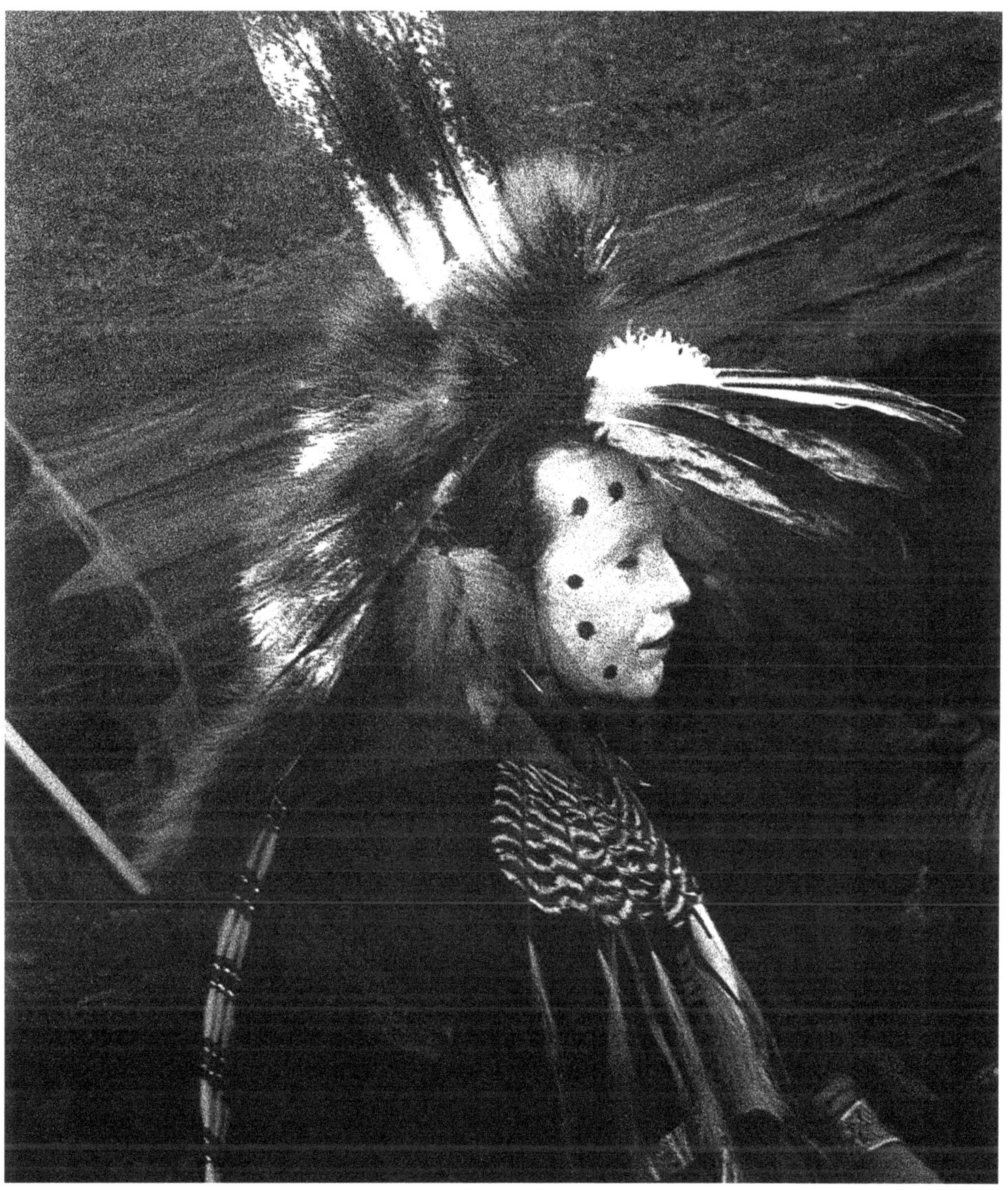

Some North American Indians have produced an artifact called a dream catcher. The commercial version is fashioned from a small willow hoop filled with an imitation spider's web woven out of colored yarn. Sometimes feathers and beads are used for decoration outside the net, but the working area must remain empty for dream collection.

Intrigued by the concept, and outmaneuvered by a roadside vendor, I bought one in Taos, New Mexico, and threatened to hang it on our bedroom wall.

I was overruled by my wife, so the object never saw anything but the inside of a closet. One day a friend with a questionable amount of Indian heritage examined the piece and said it looked heavy with dreams.

"In fact, some of these dreams are old," he muttered while staring into the net. I said I was astonished, since the dream catcher was probably made within the past couple of years. "Doesn't Matter," my friend said, with certainty. "Dreams and visions are related, and over time either can become myth, handed down from generation to generation. The dreams in this net could have originated from visions of the net makers great, great grandfather."

In fact, my friend proclaimed, "This net contains a mixture of Indian dreams and white man delusions. Some are pure, and others resemble Ricardo Montalban in headdress and war paint."

My friend and I, however, were full of firewater, and at least one of us was delusional. But the truth is that I hope some of my dreams are contained in the net.

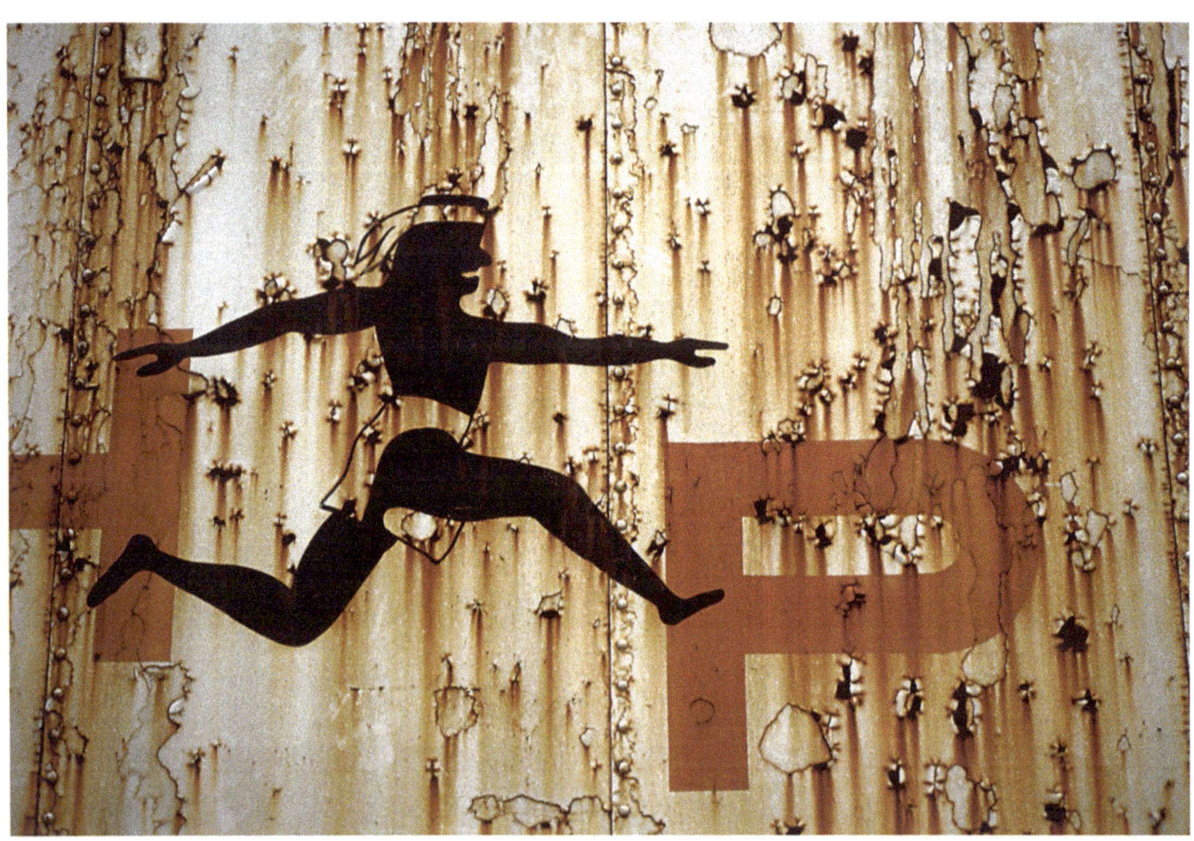

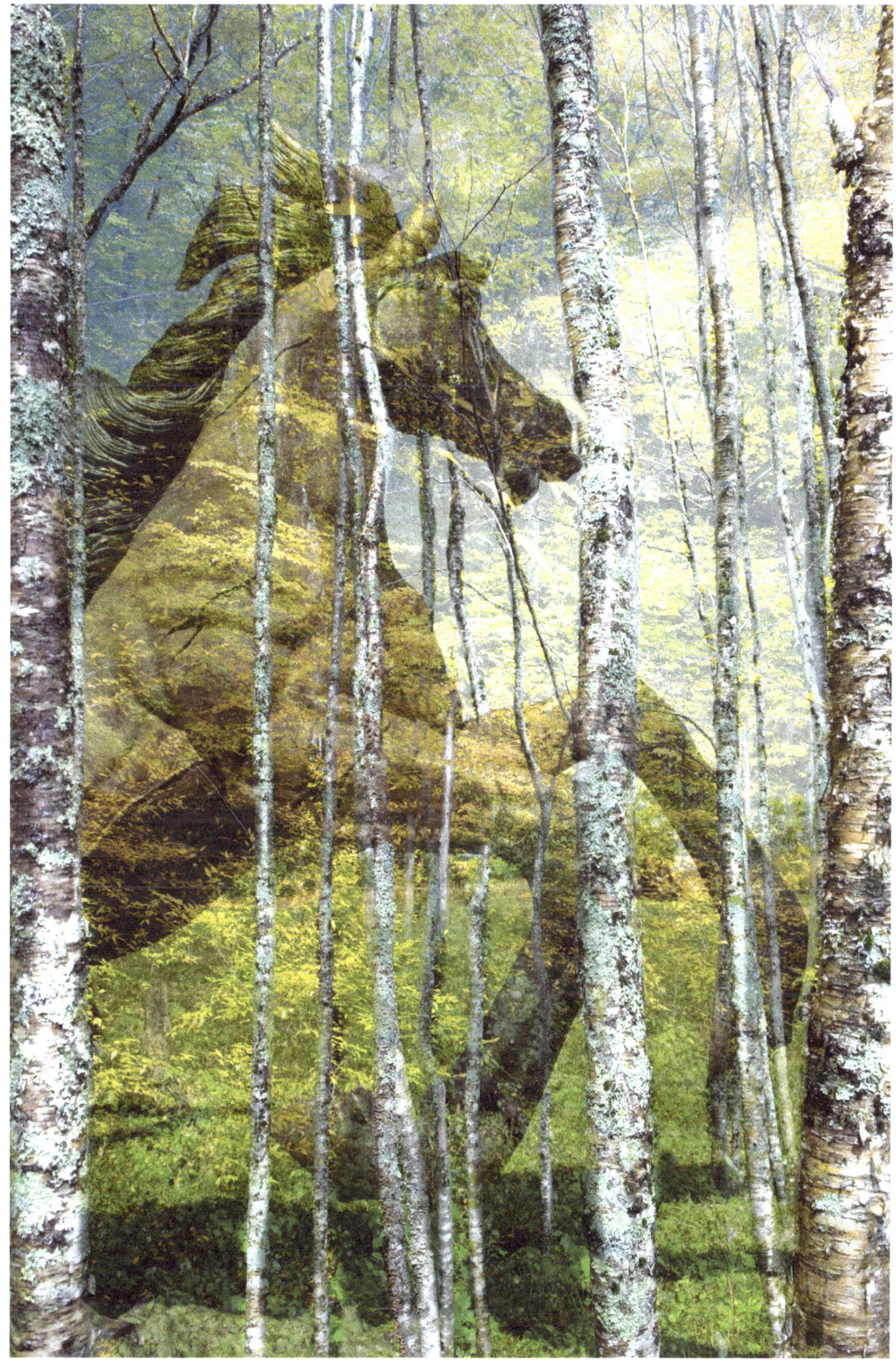

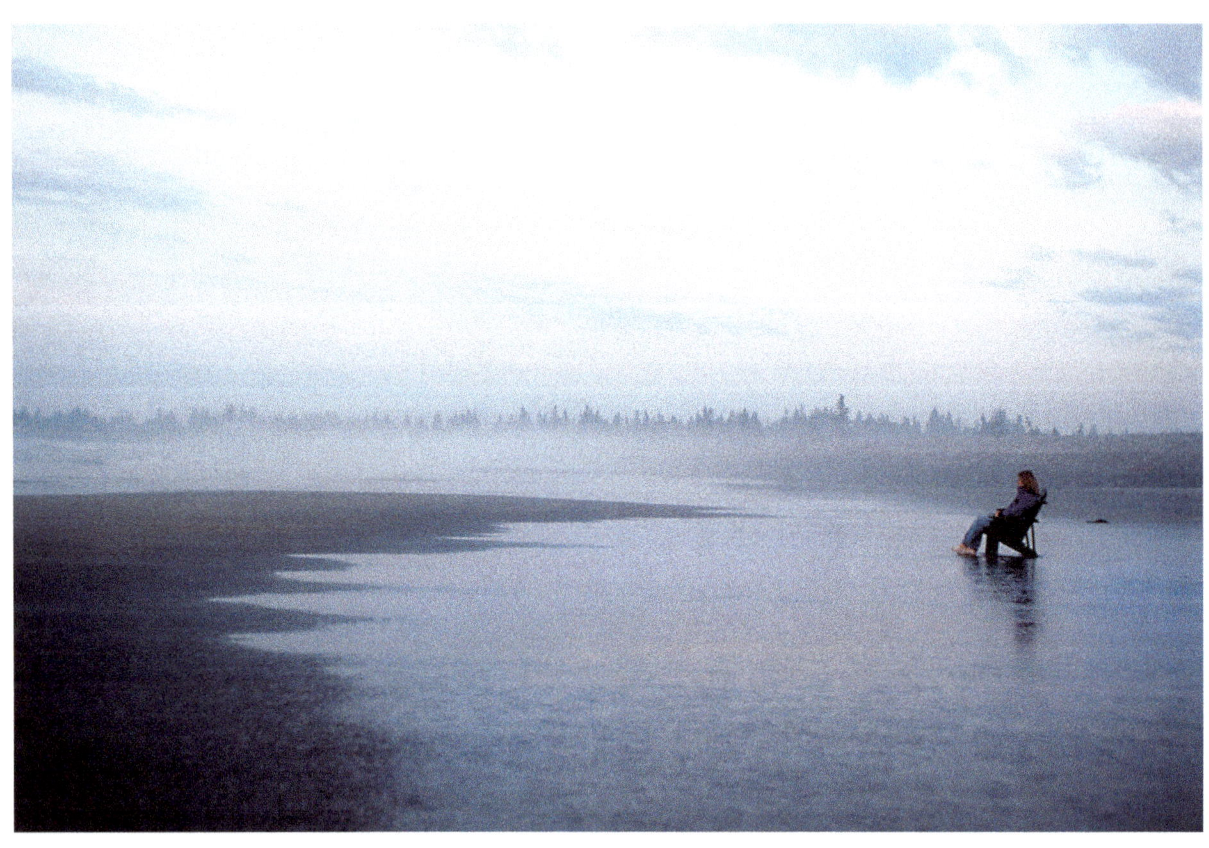

Brain scans suggest that the mind in slumber works about the same as when awake, but a part of the brain takes its own nap. The prefrontal cortex, which controls caution and clear thinking, goes dormant during sleep.

When that happens, language and logic become less important, and visual creativity moves to the forefront. Noradrenalin and serotonin allow the brain to perform tasks, solve problems, and remember things. Those chemicals are absent during REM sleep, which accounts for why it is sometimes hard to remember dreams.

The most profound dream I ever had was probably drug-induced. It happened during my second night home from the hospital after knee surgery. I was on pain pills and antihistamines, trying to sleep propped up in bed because that was the most comfortable position.

There were no people, places, or events in the dream. Instead of a story I saw a formula, a combination of letters and numbers that represented the way to never make a wrong decision. The formula was simple, maybe four or five single digit numbers, each one followed by a letter. I believe the number-letter combinations represented various ways of looking at any given situation. It looked something like this: 1R7Q3U9B.

Finding the formula was accompanied by a sense of good fortune. I had obtained something of great importance, and it made perfect sense.

Then the knowledge slowly began to dissolve, like a thought slipping away. I directed all my concentration at the formula, but some outside force was pulling the enlightenment away, keeping it just outside my mind's grasp.

The real world began to intrude as I slowly realized I was drenched in sweat, and the dull pain from my surgery began to eat through my dream.

I was losing the formula and its meaning.

Quickly, I found my pen and notepad on the nightstand and wrote down everything I could remember.

Some important information must have slipped away, though, because I've made several wrong decisions since then.

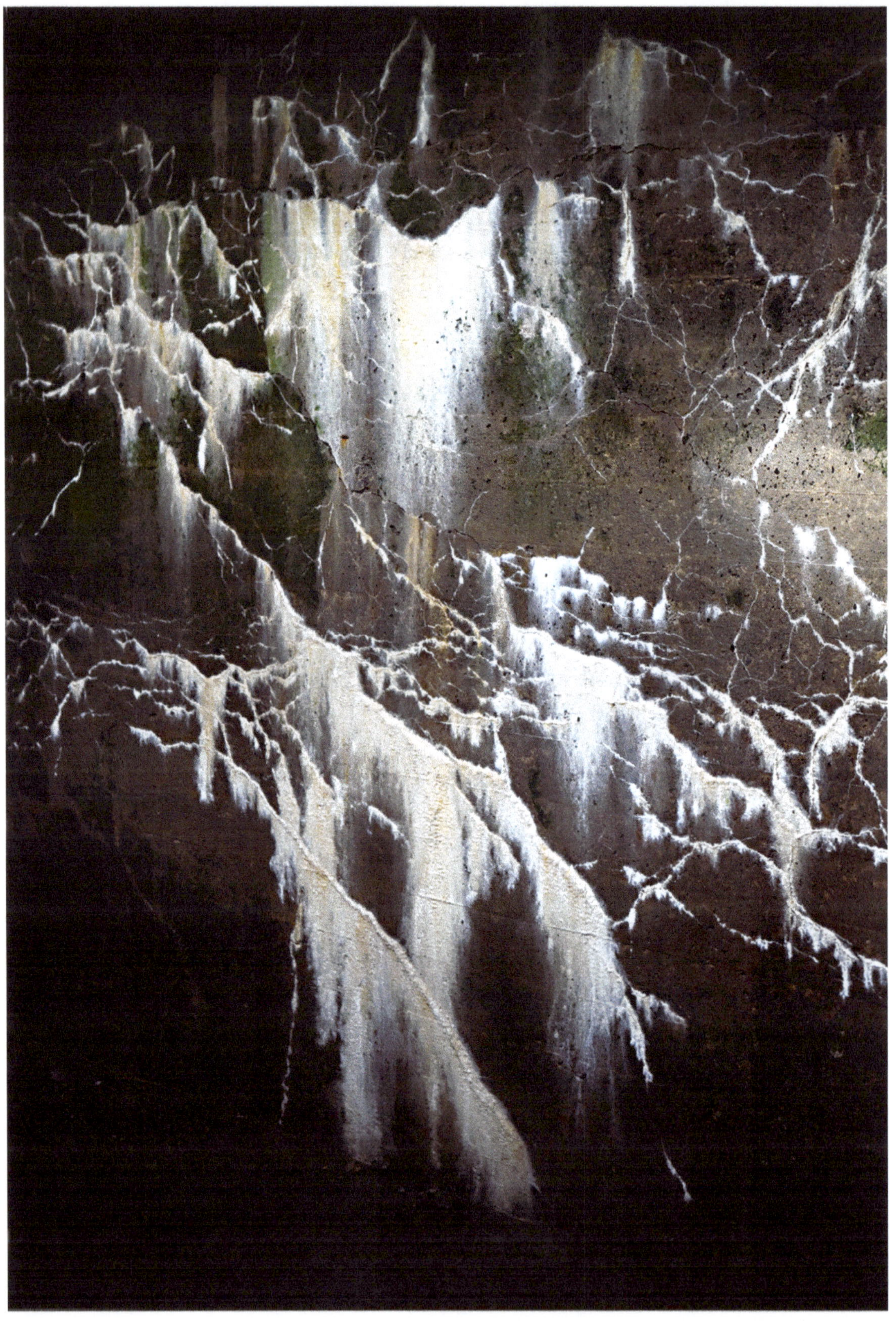

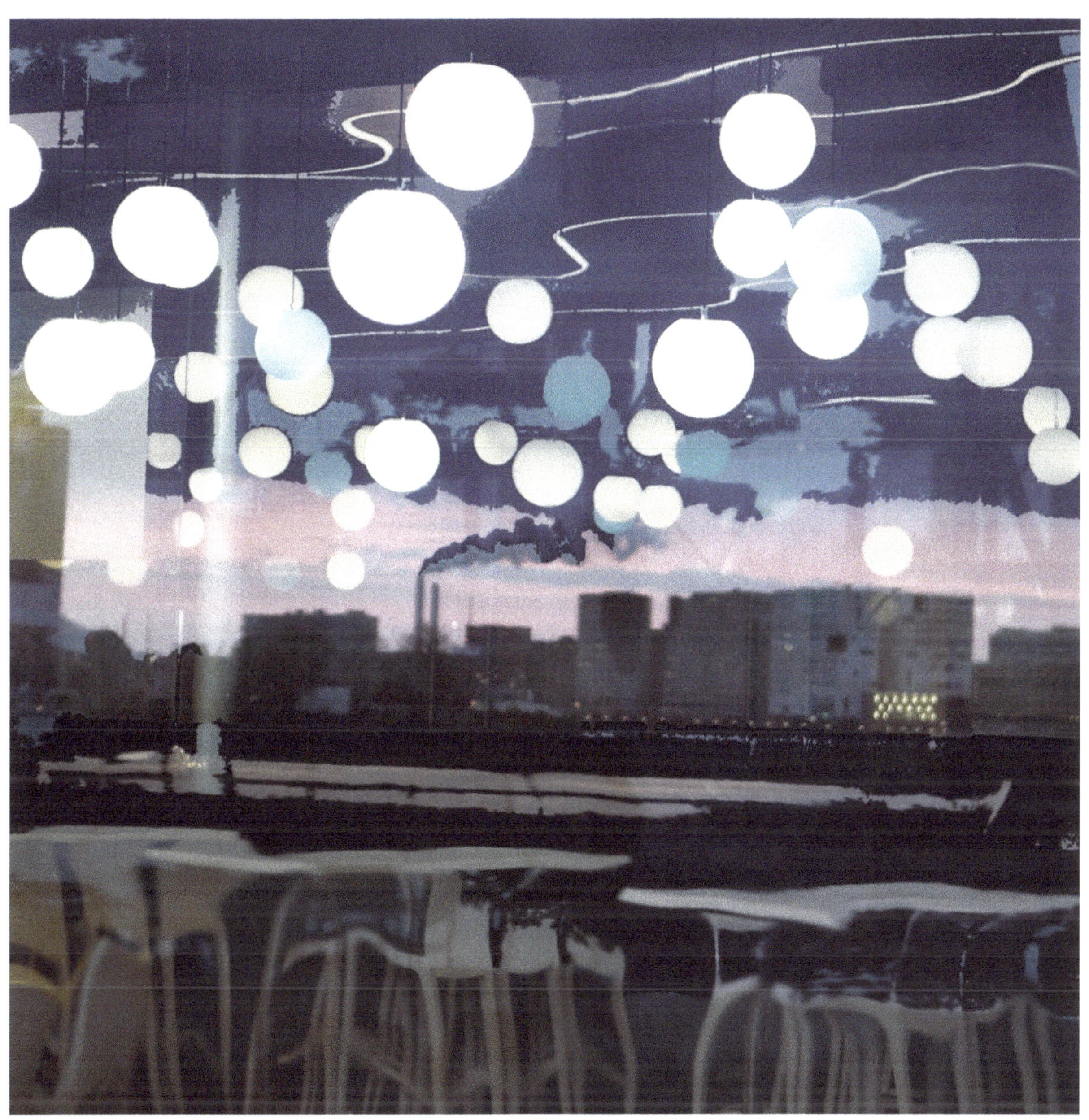

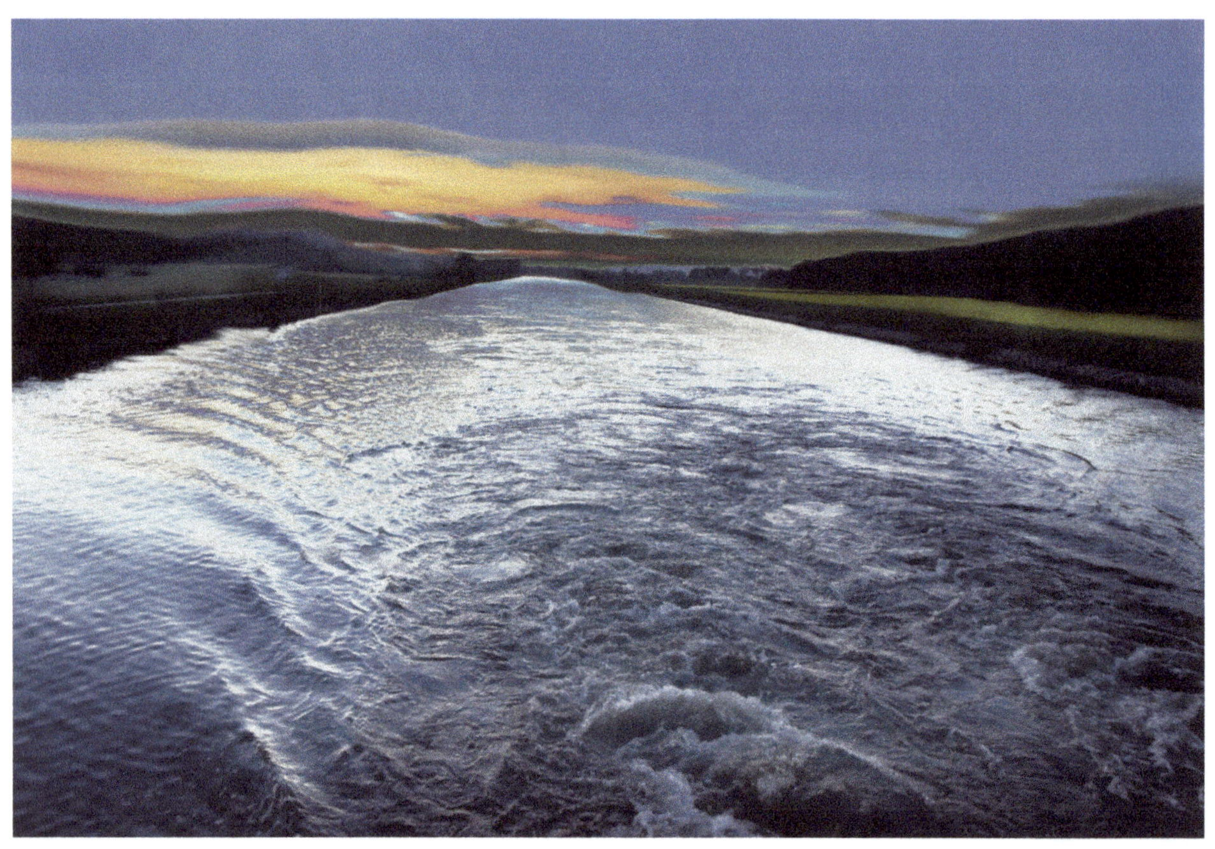

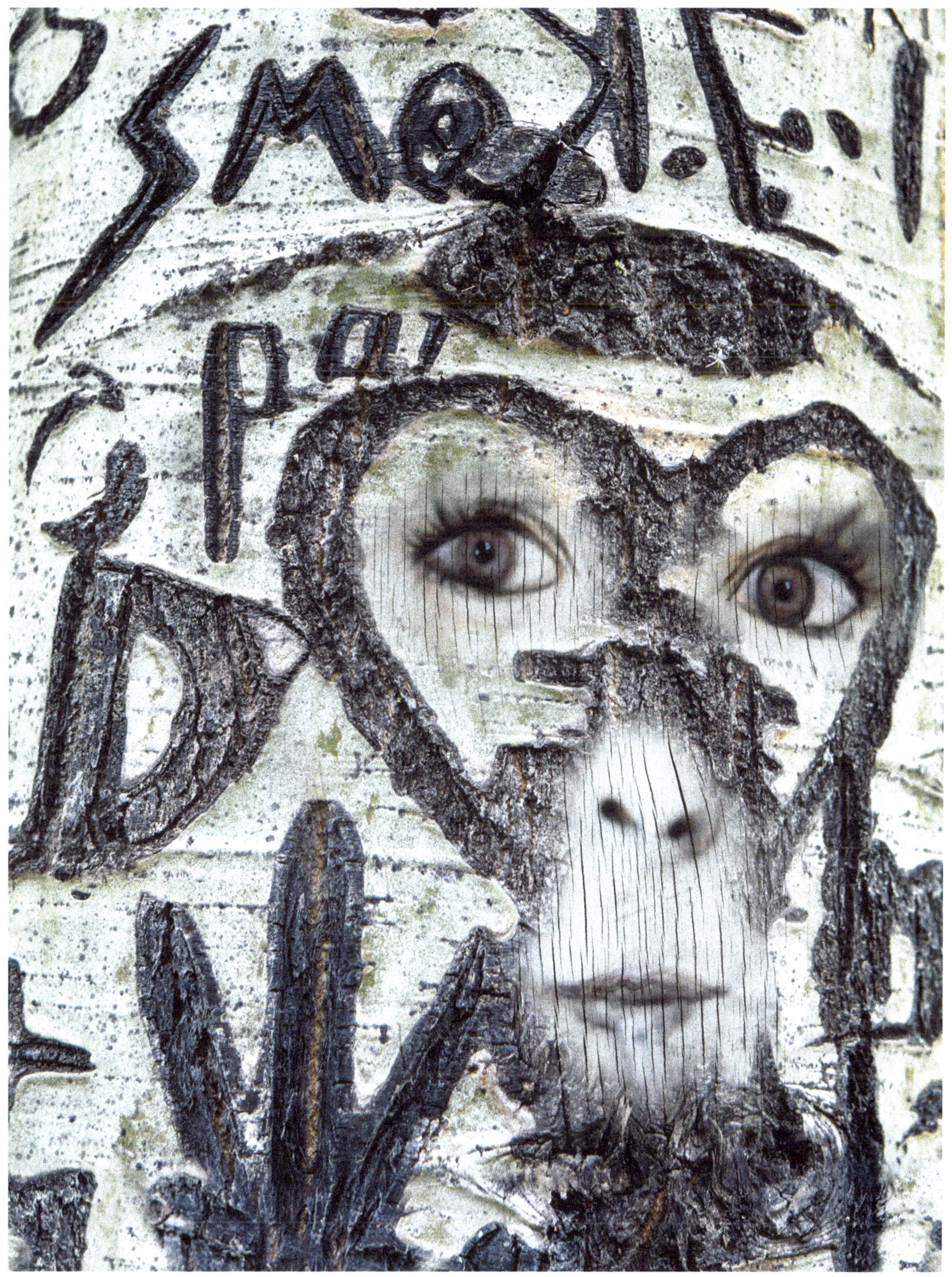

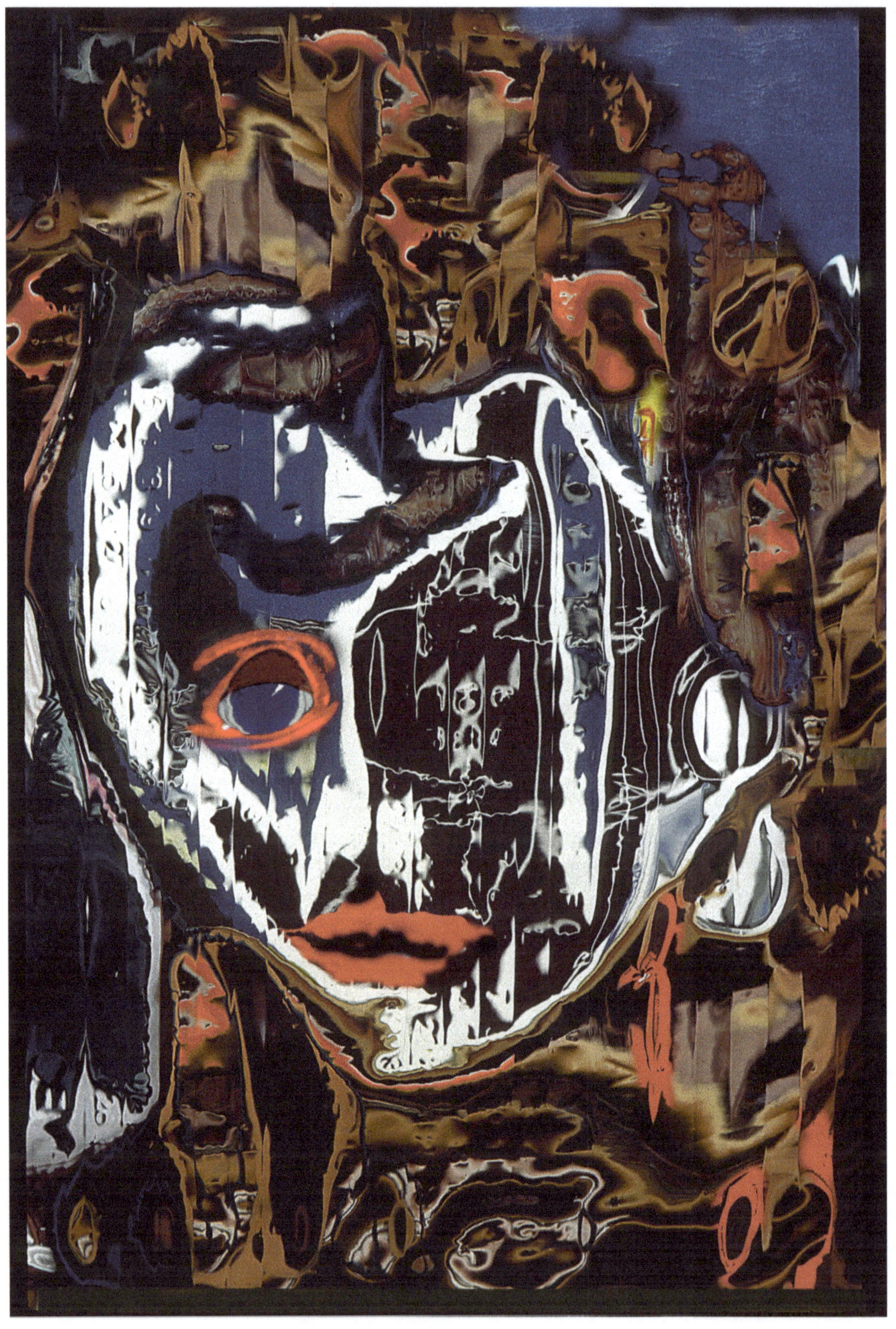

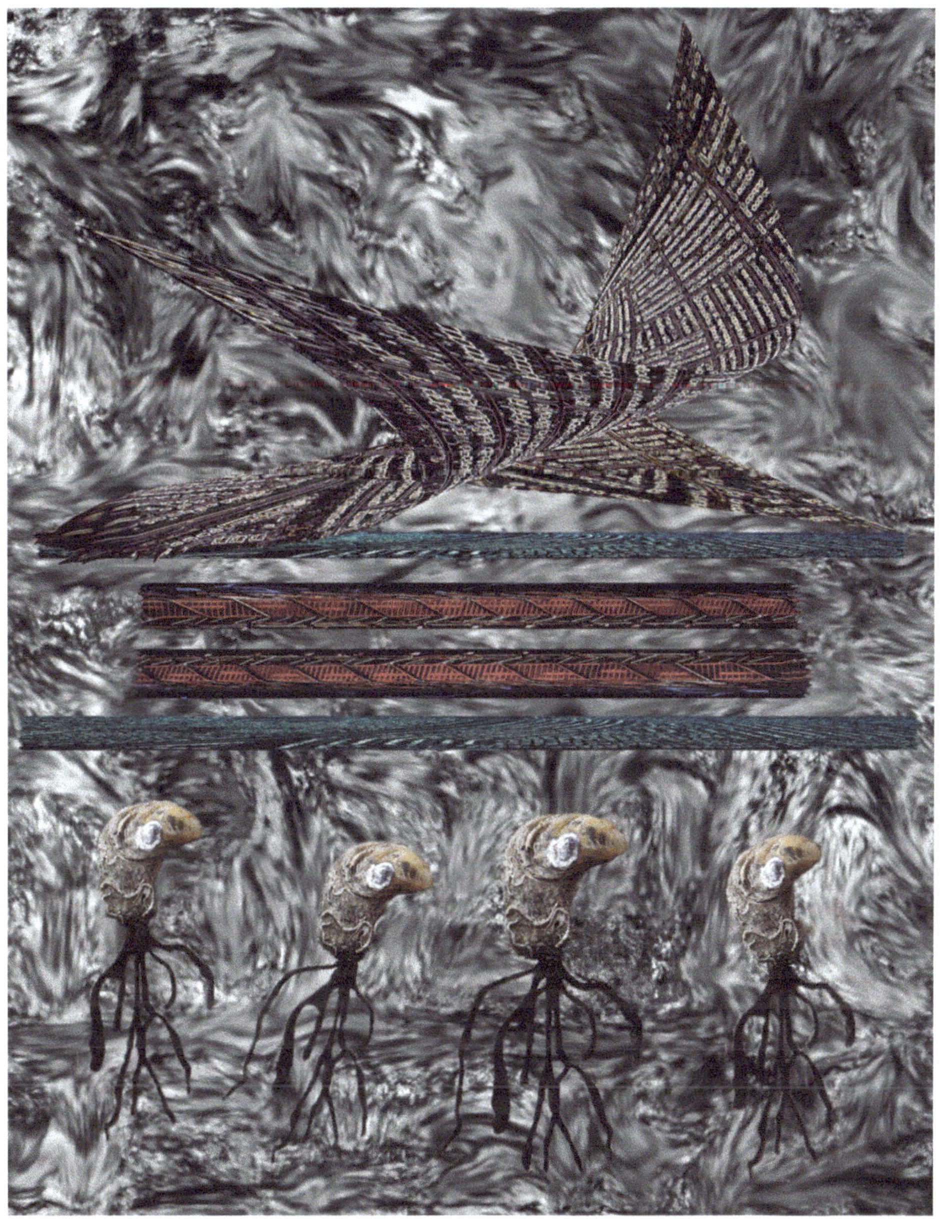

I found a shell in low tide. Strands of seaweed that resembled body protrusions were attached to one side.

That night the shell crept back into my subconscious and brought some friends. They were "supposedly" of a higher intelligence than ours, but you could not tell it by the way they carried themselves.

They appeared to be involved in some form of data worship, but the scene reminded me of an alien parade.

Occasionally, daytime information filters back into our dreams in a different context. Our brains produce more images than our eyes will ever see.

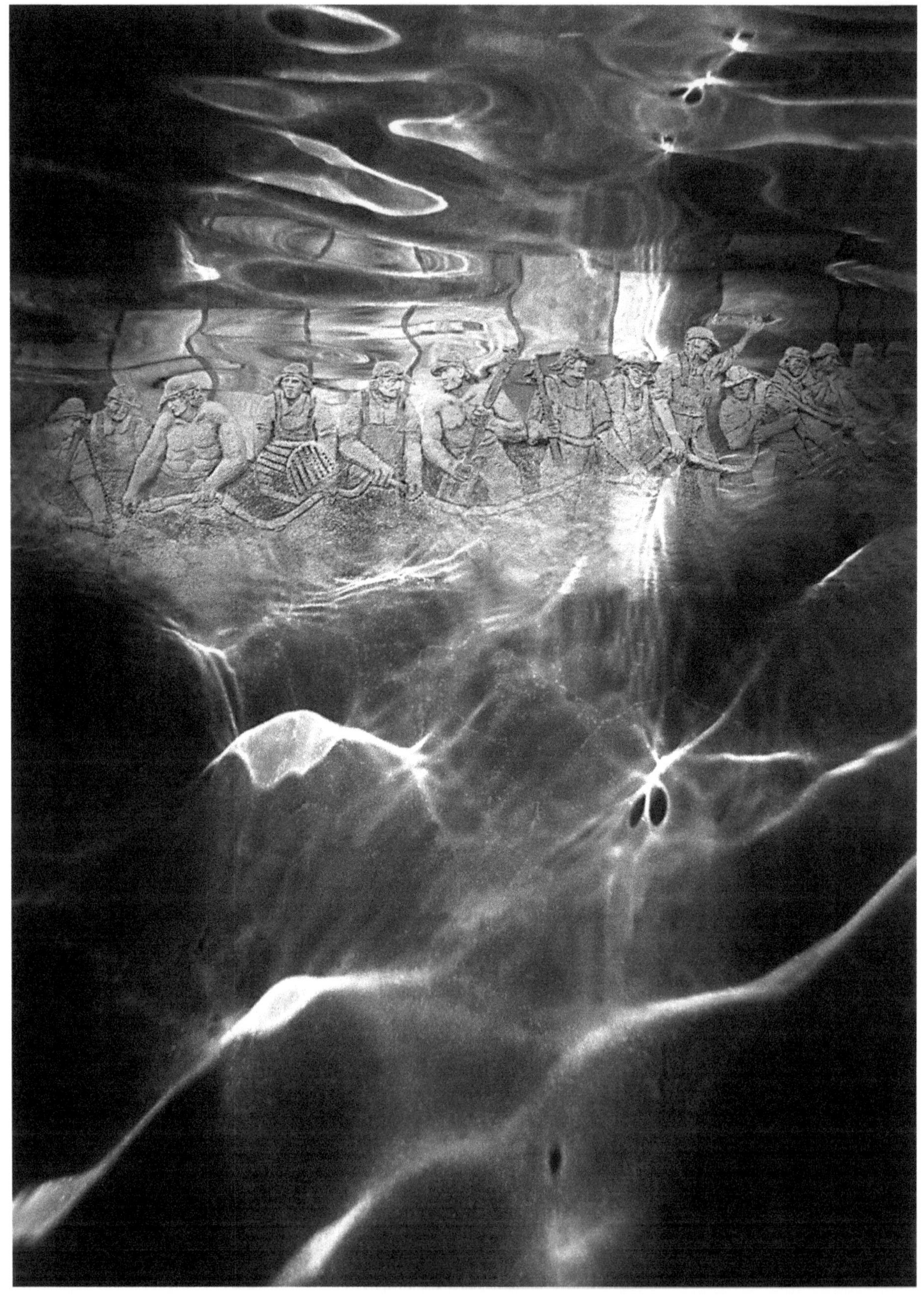

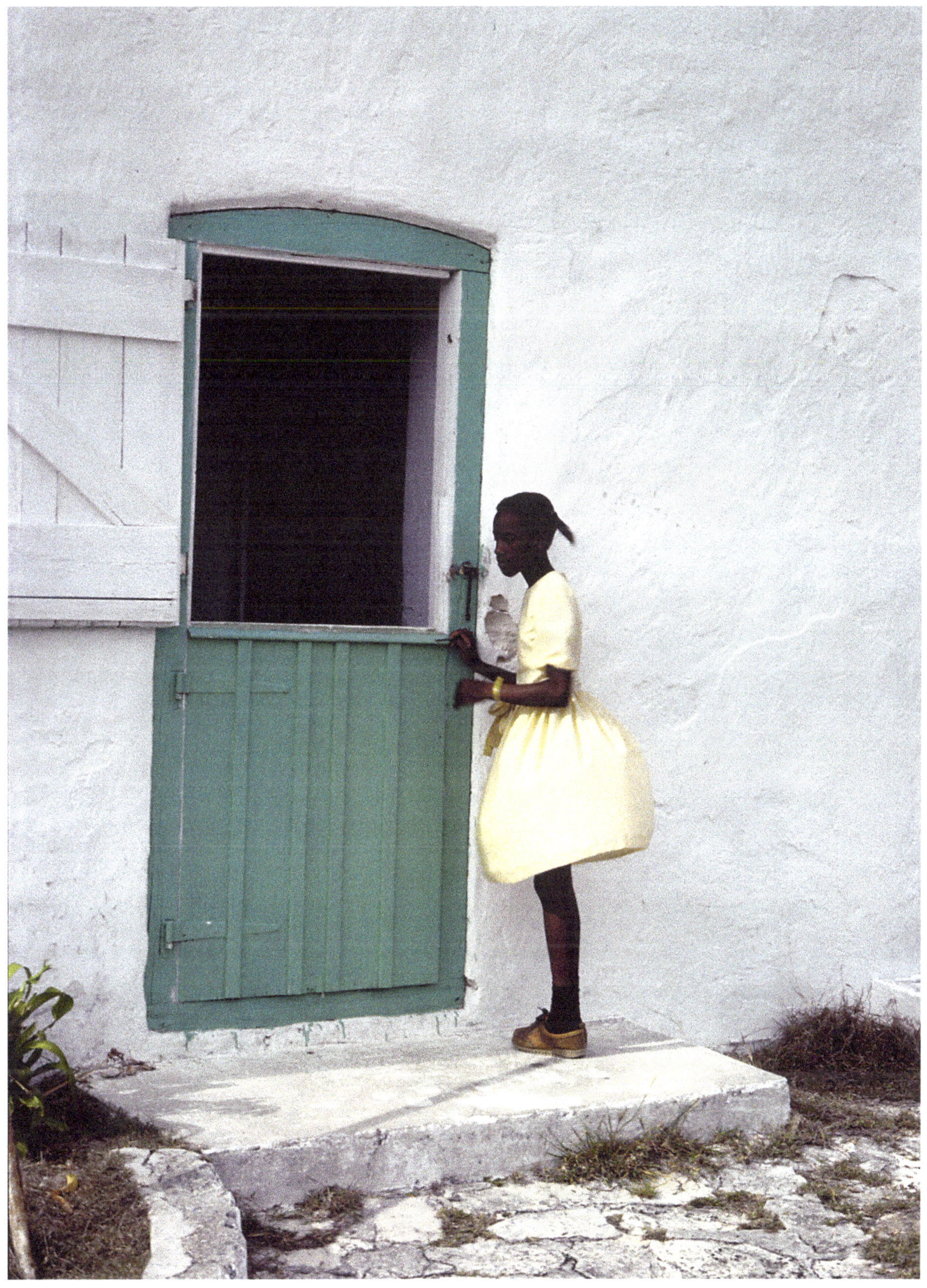

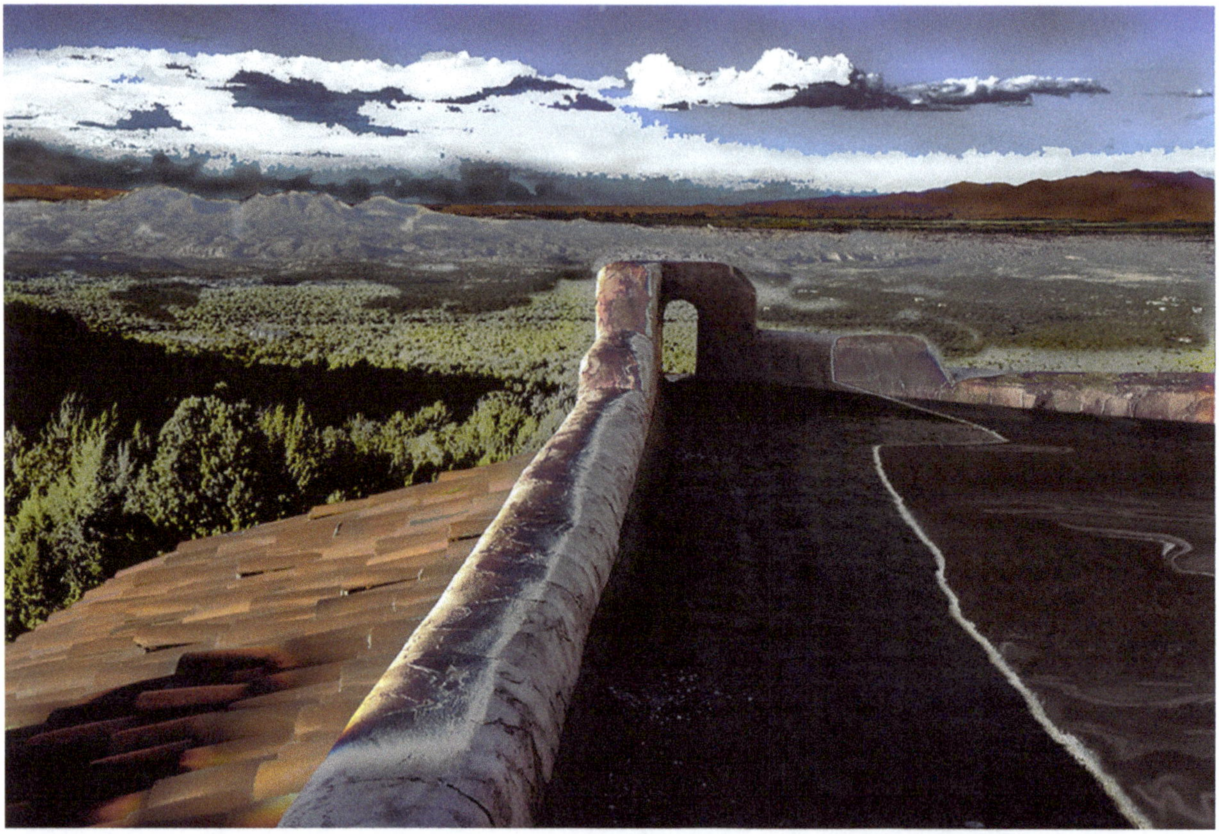

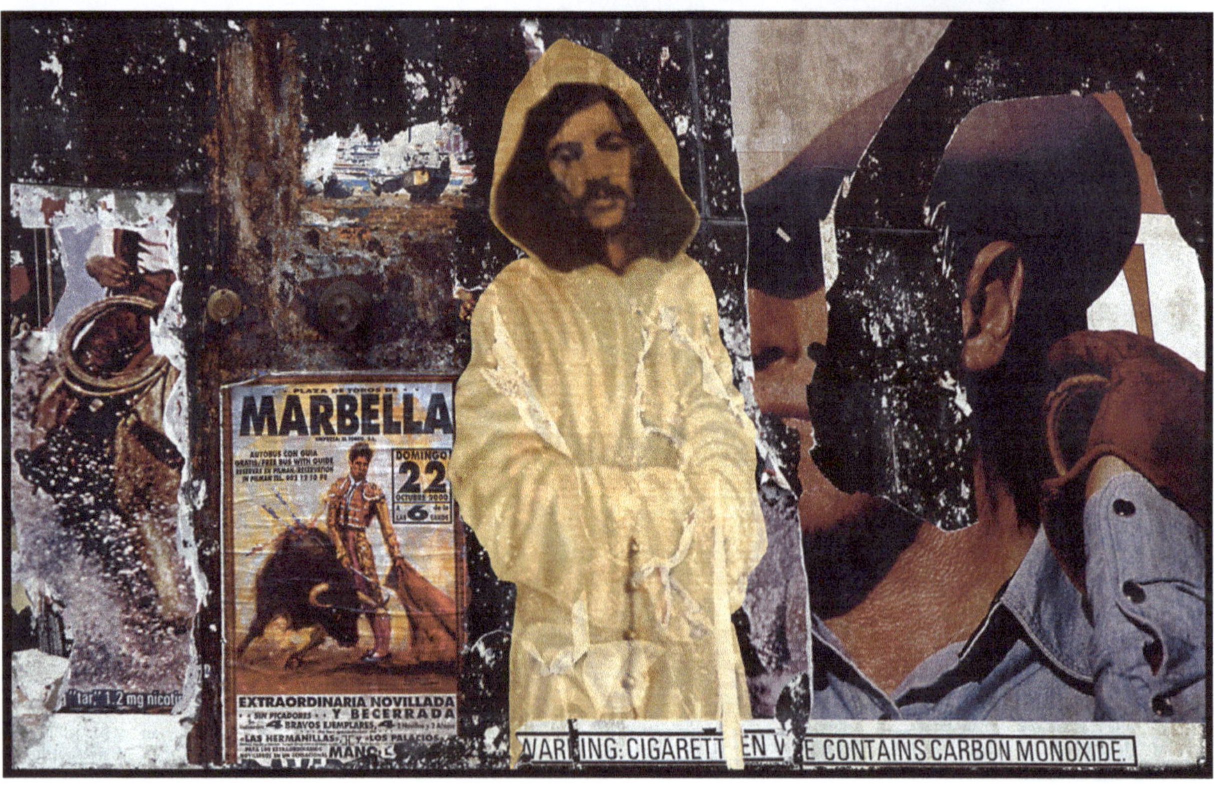
PLAZA DE TOROS DE
MARBELLA
AUTOBUS CON GUIA
GRATIS/FREE BUS WITH GUIDE
DOMINGO
22
OCTUBRE 2000
6
EXTRAORDINARIA NOVILLADA
SIN PICADORES
Y BECERRADA
4 BRAVOS EJEMPLARES, 4
«LAS HERMANILLAS» y «LOS PALACIOS»
"tar," 1.2 mg nicoti
WAR ING: CIGARETT EN V E CONTAINS CARBON MONOXIDE.

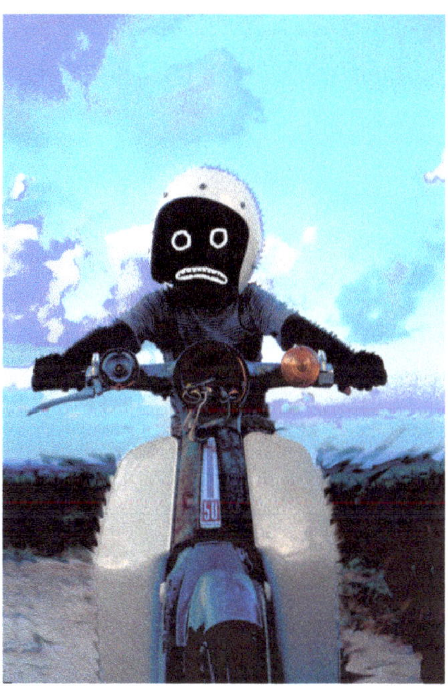

In some dreams I am myself, but other times I am just an observer with no body and no place in the action.

When I do make an appearance, my dream persona is younger, more agile, and has more hair than the real me. I have never dreamed of myself as the older person I have become. People I am familiar with retain their younger appearances as well. My wife, parents, and some close friends are always recognizable, even if they seem like younger apparitions of their present-day selves.

Still other dream characters seem to have absolutely no physical constraints or limitations. They are real people I have met or seen in waking life but do not know enough about for my nocturnal mind to make any firm conclusions. Like the late shift at an all-night party, these creations become more bizarre as sleep progresses. The deep sleep or rapid-eye-movement (REM) cycles generally happen toward the end of sleep. During REM sleep these visual impersonations make an appearance. The guest list can include caricatures of real people, and monsters, (one of which was patterned after the creature from the black lagoon, who made an indelible impression on me many years ago). Some are animals of mixed species, and underwater creatures that need no imaginary help to seem bizarre.

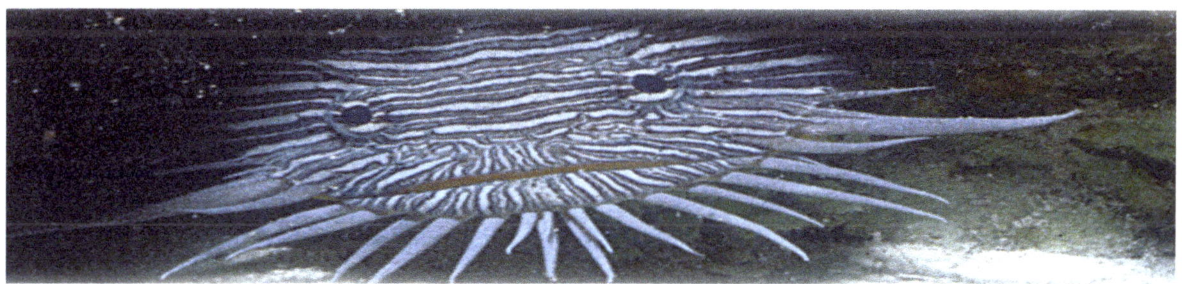

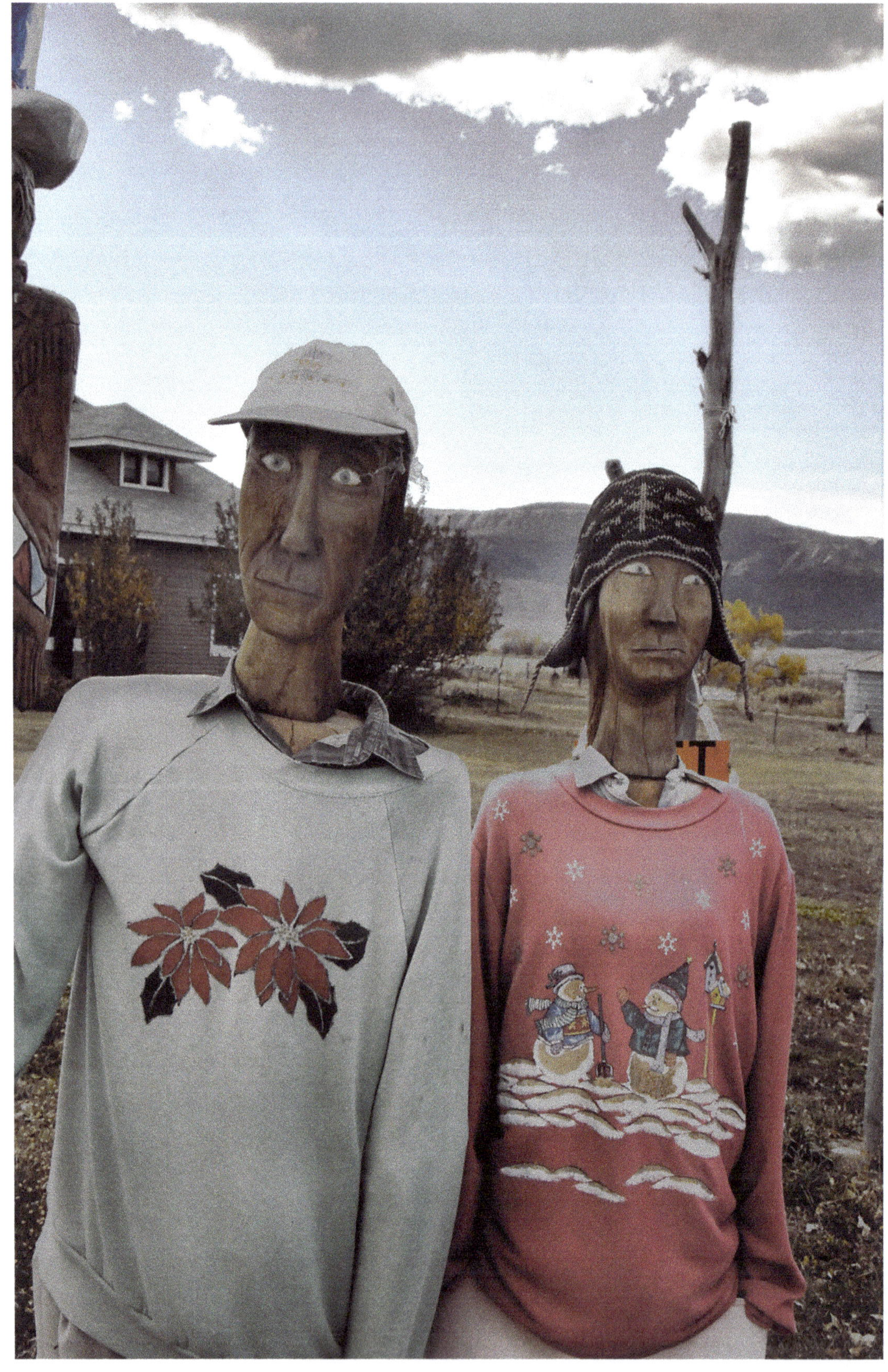

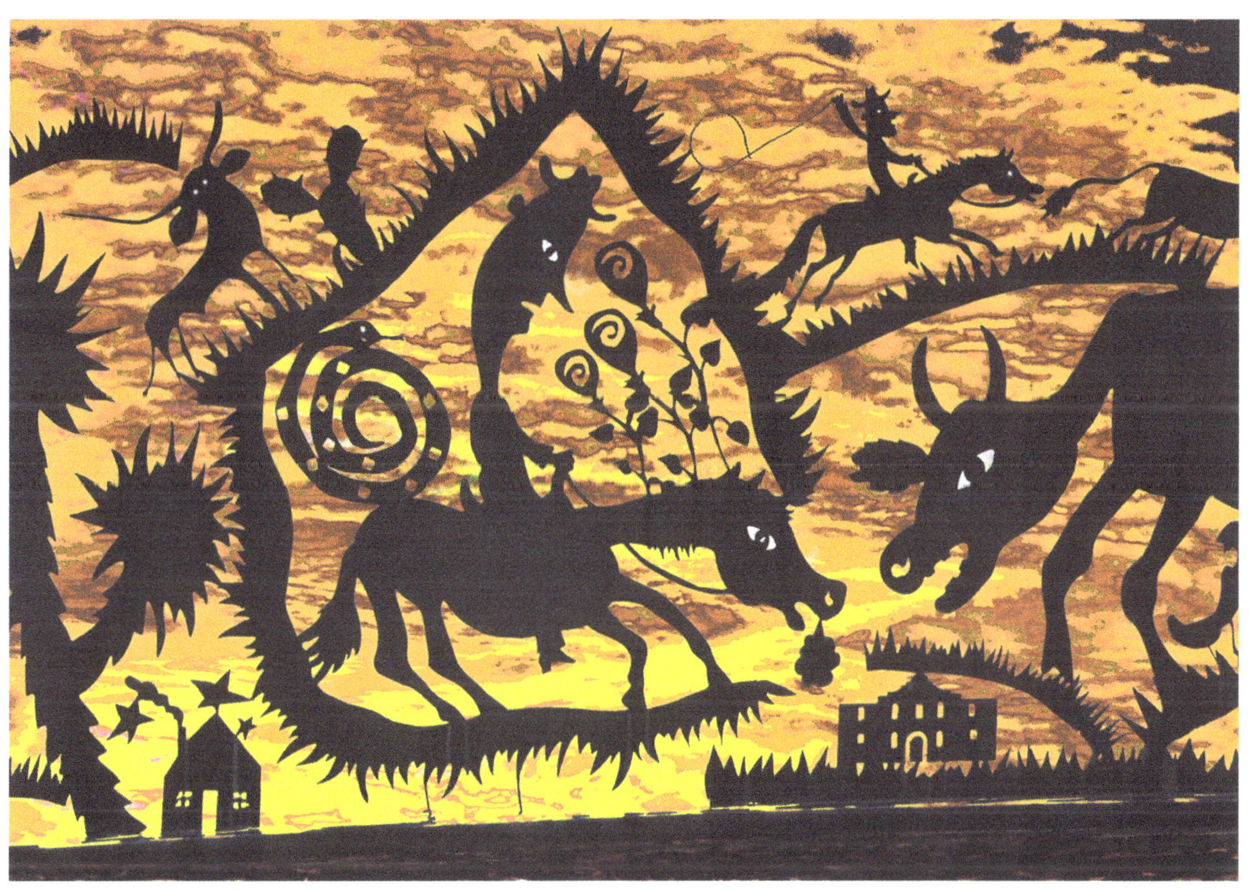

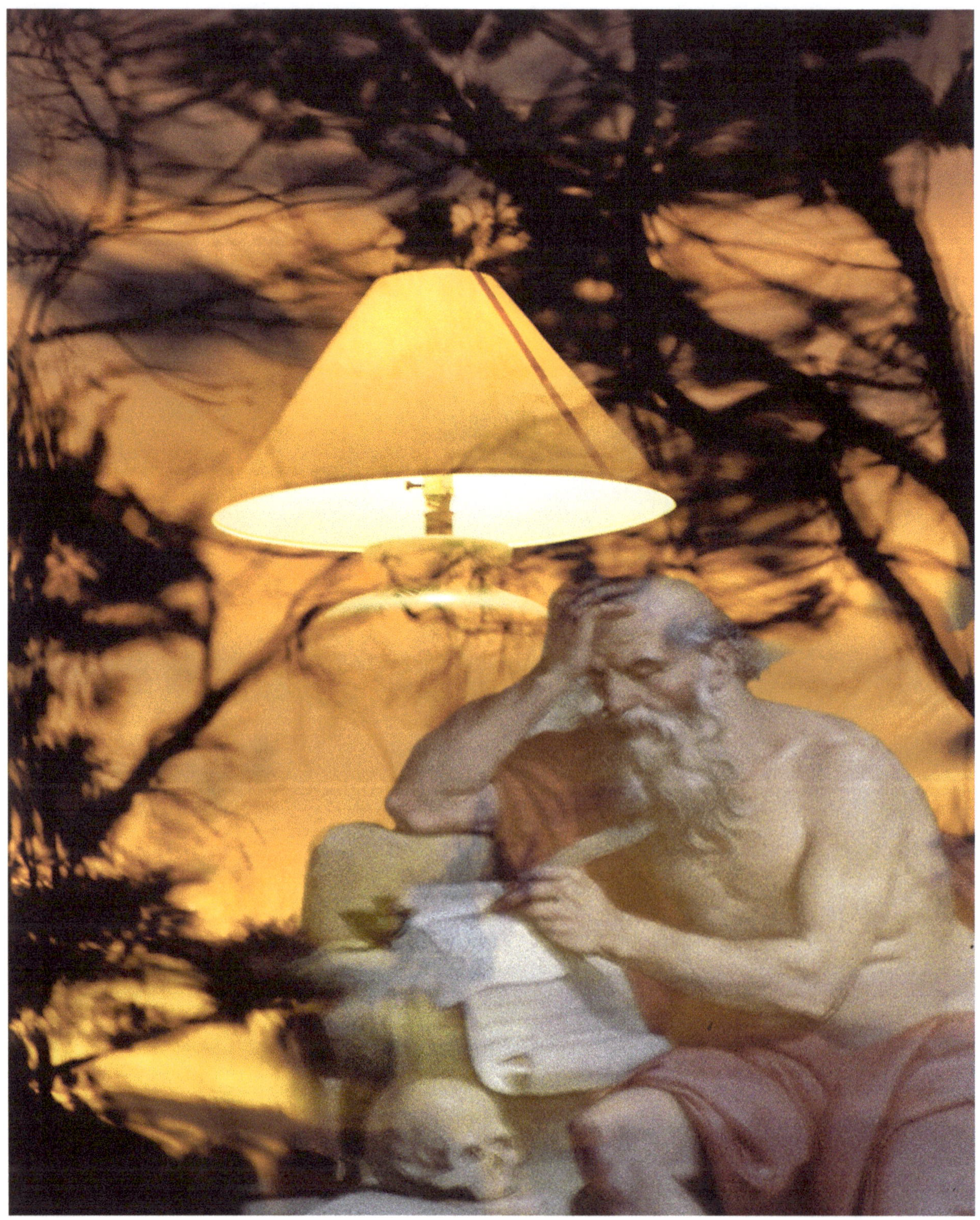

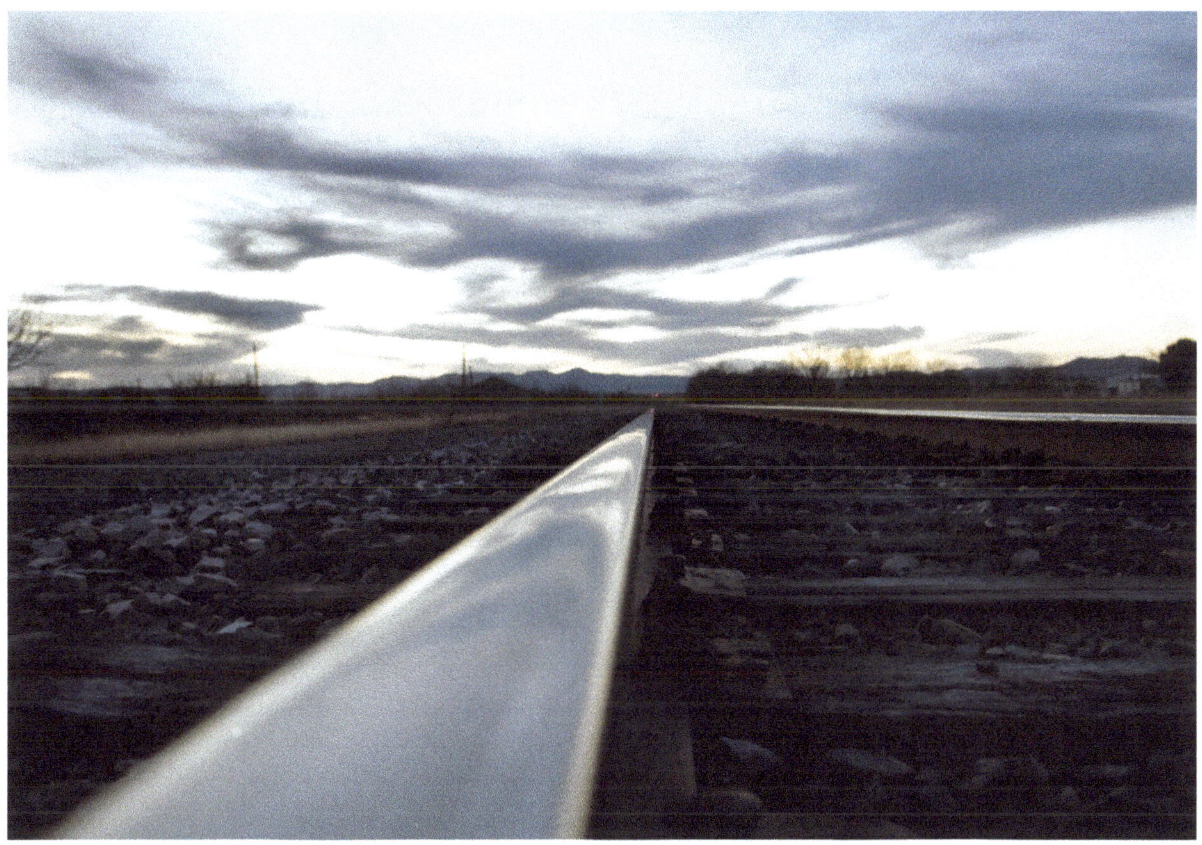

Travel was my dream pursuit. It was the thing I would do when time and money became more accessible. The conventional trips I managed to take only left me wanting more. I went from point A to point B on numerous occasions, using ordinary means of transportation.

But cars, trains, and airplanes are light years from the process I use to get around now. Not until I learned to leave my body at home did I really begin to travel.

One night I fell asleep and dreamed about astral projection. My consciousness was sliding through a static landscape, similar to what you might see by looking out the side window of a speeding car. There was no real feeling of movement other than the visual effect caused by a blurred vista. Something in the rush of scenery caught my eye. It was some sort of an opening, but it flew by so fast that all that was left was its image imprinted on my brain. I willed myself to stop, and return. It was a portal, surrounded by the basic elements of earth, water, and sky. The center was dark and inviting, and since it existed only within a dream, I stepped inside.

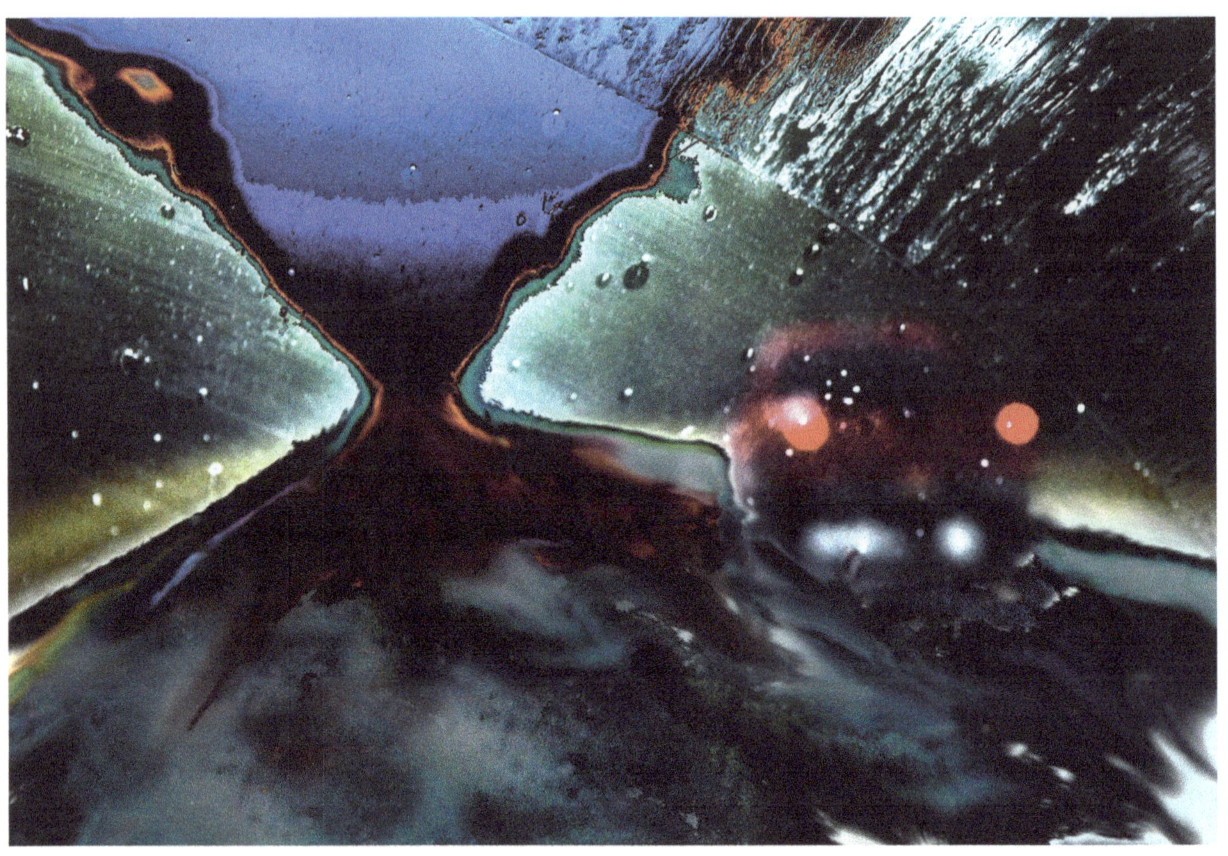

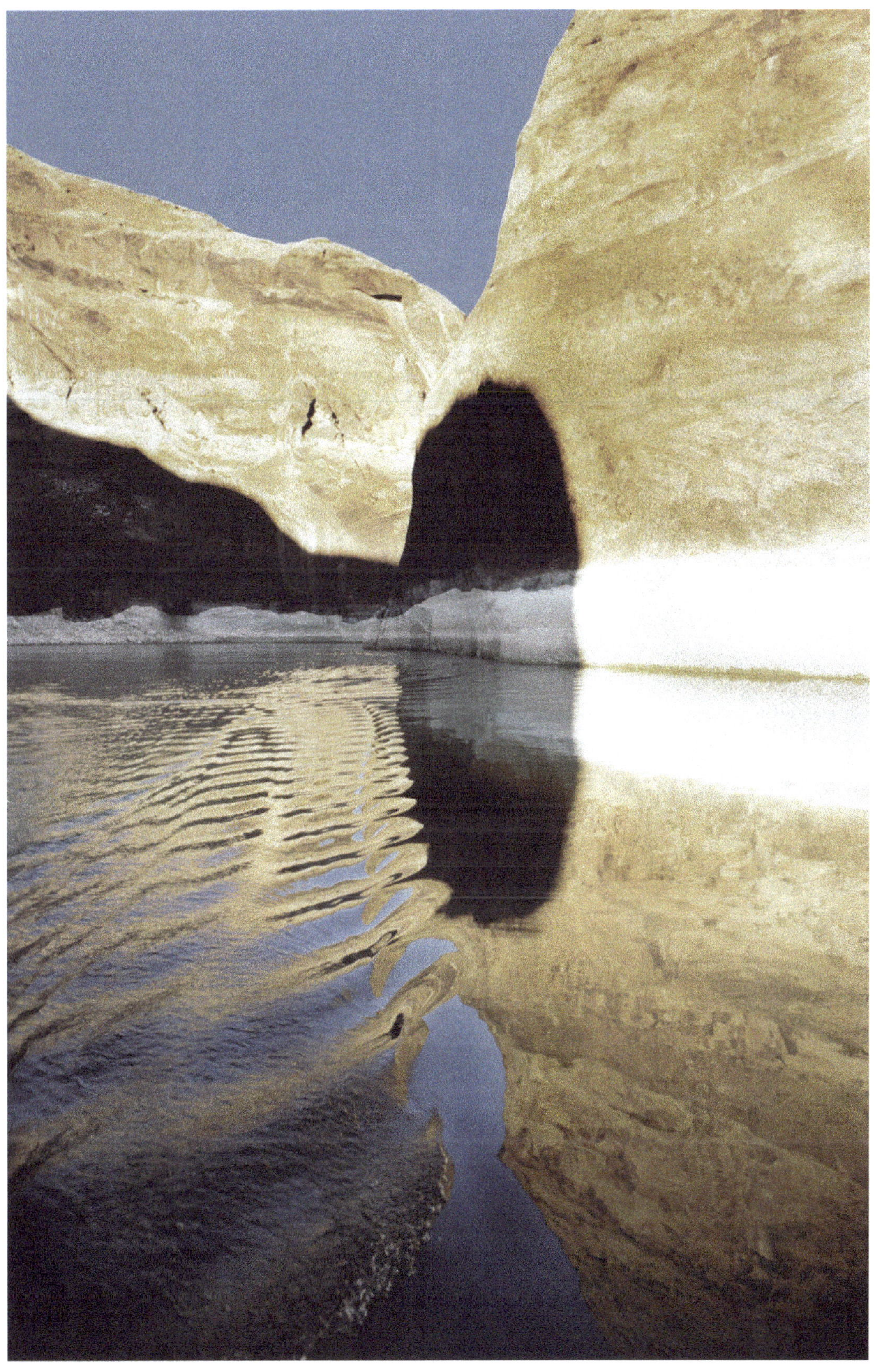

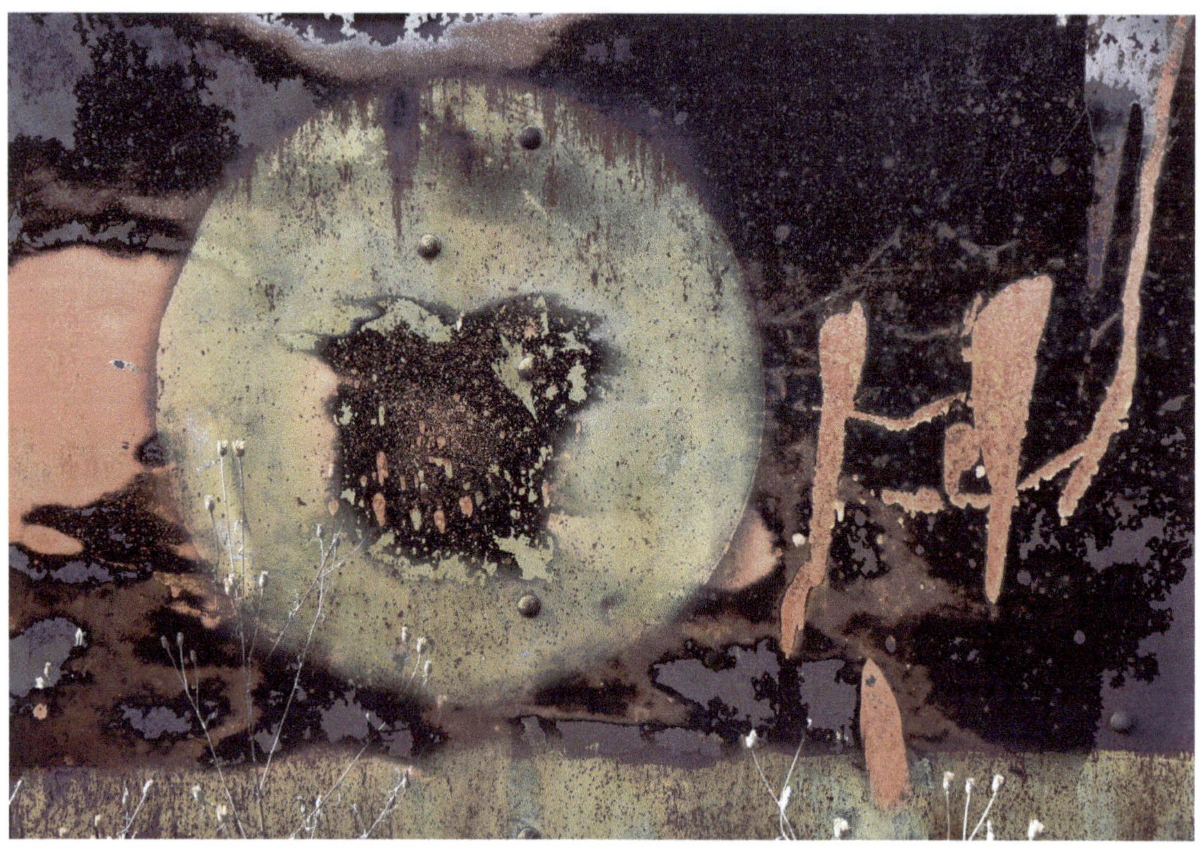

The opening led to another dimension, or perhaps some previously undetected level of my own consciousness. The rules of dream world did not apply there, so I could not will myself awake. Also, the portal was a one-way passage, which is to say the inside looked nothing like the outside, and even if it had, I doubted I could pass back through. So my new objective was to find another portal and hope it would lead back home. Time did exist there, because I saw the sun rise and set on numerous occasions, sometimes in rapid succession. In any case, I was there long enough to realize the way out was not in this general vicinity. I was on the move again, looking for a way back home. The initial excitement of transmigration faded. It felt a lot like dream travel, and I was certain my body was at home in bed, resting peacefully, even as my eyes twitched rapidly under closed lids. This might have been a dream about astral projection, but it was still a dream, and the only way to end it was by awakening. I was more or less in control of events, and even though I did not need a body just to transport my mind from place to place, I usually do have one that changes according to some unknown rule of metaphysics. Great leaps of distance are better accomplished without a body, but that also increases the chance of missing the exit to reality. I prefer a body for shorter distances, and those with four legs seem to have more stamina.

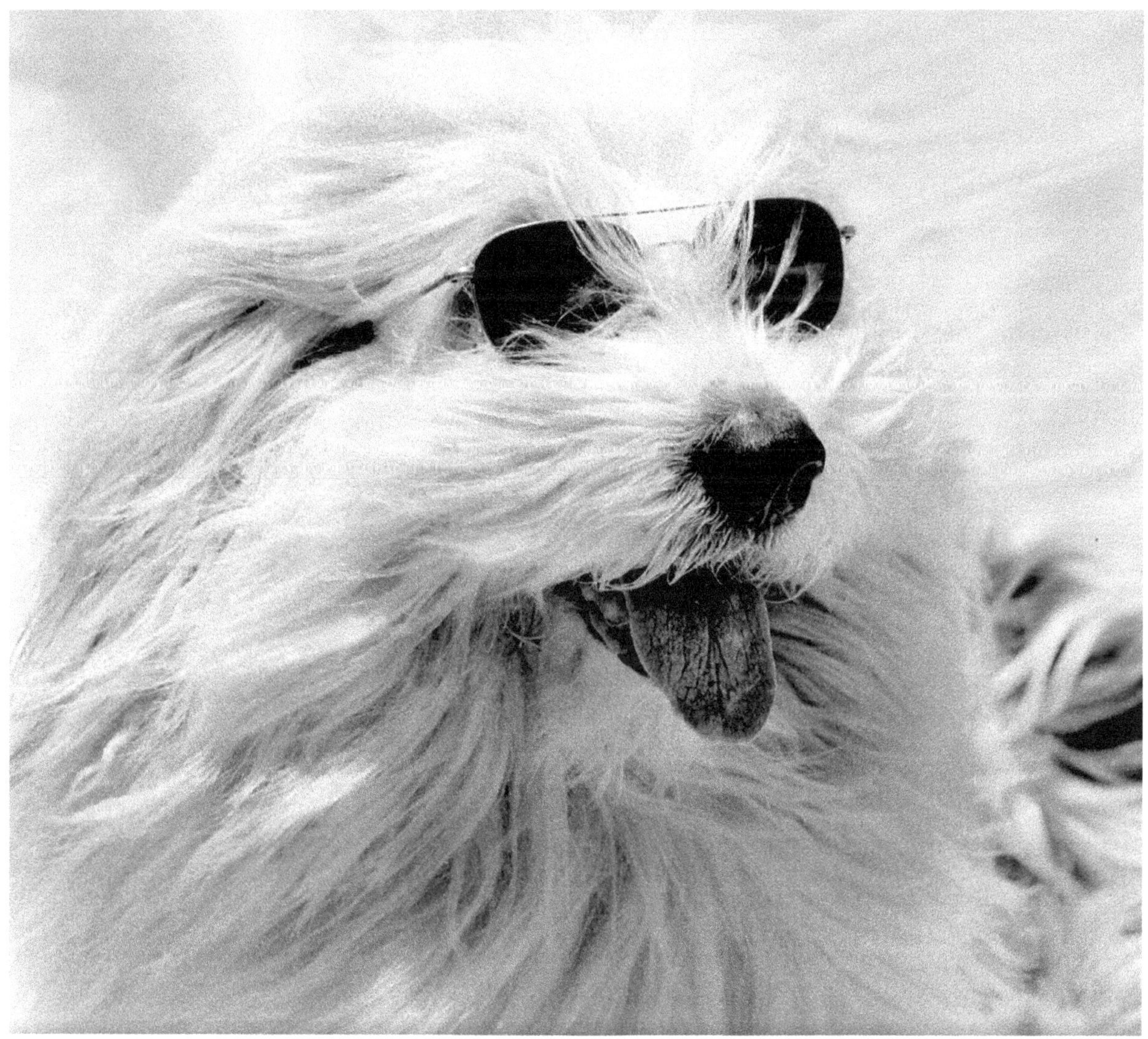

So I became a dog and remained that way long enough to infuse my mind with primal urges that could cause problems when I re-attained human form. All species have basic instincts, and they deal with them in their own way. Realizing what is and is not acceptable public behavior highlights one mental cavern, and the urge to travel reveals another. Dogs go elsewhere because they are led in a certain direction, usually by their noses. Humans are more complicated. They sometimes travel for fun, or because they have never been to a certain place before. I do not know of another species that does that. No doubt I would readjust when the time came.

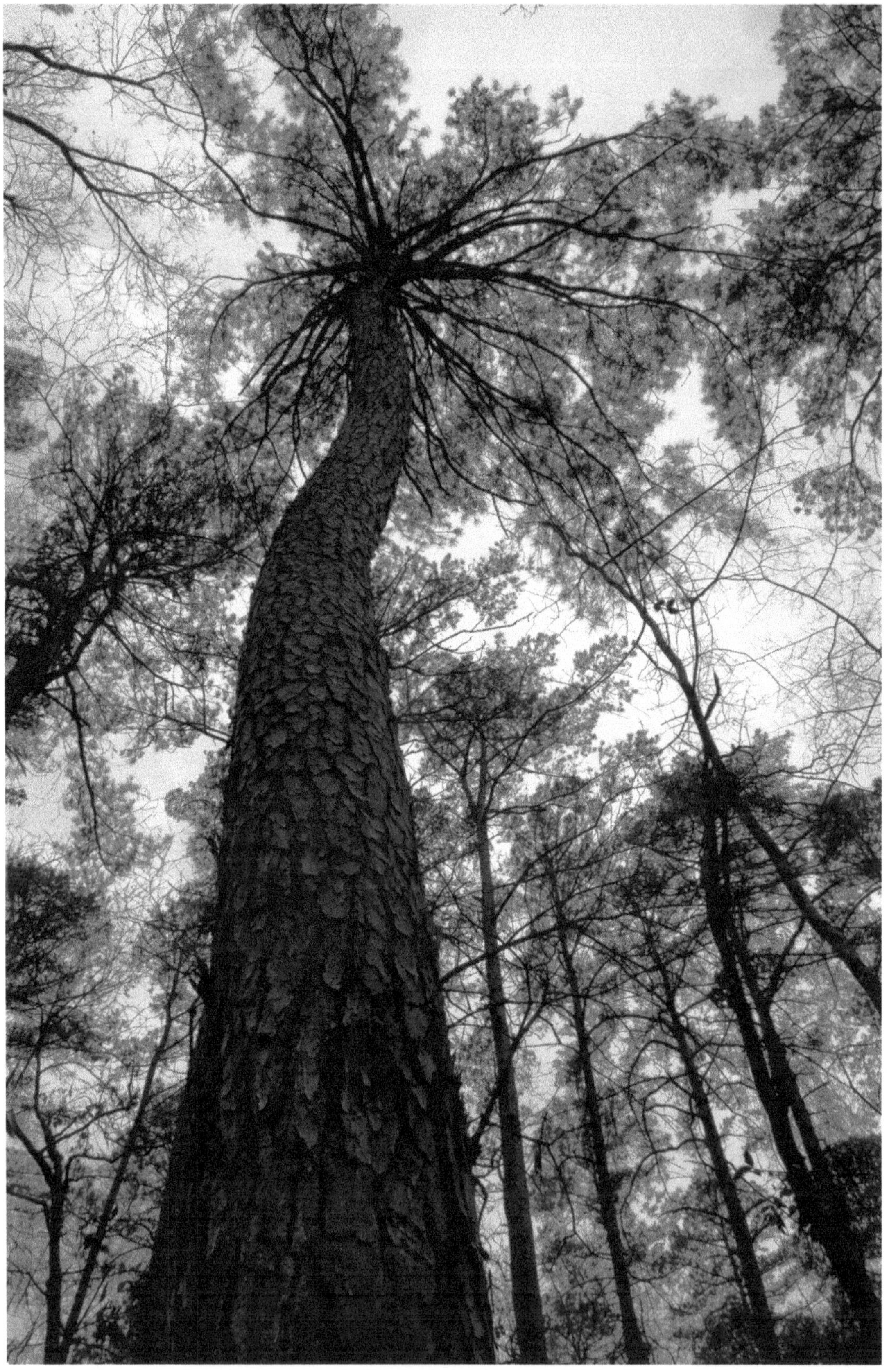

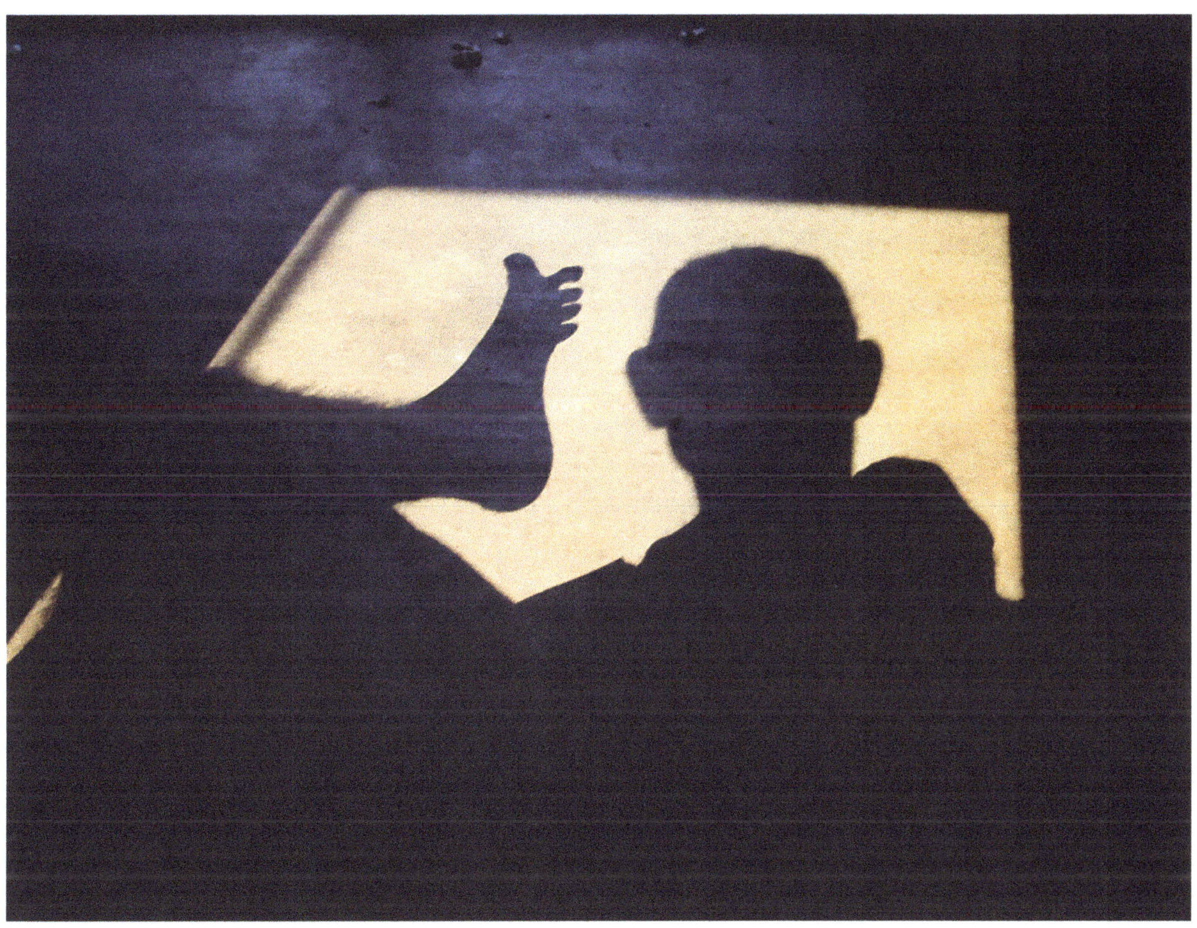

Then one day in Peru, standing atop of the Andes, I saw a llama and realized I had no desire to chase it. Looking down I could see I was bipedal, probably human. The situation was improving. Furthermore, it felt as if I had traveled back into a more familiar state of mind. I was still living and interacting with beings that resided nowhere but within my imagination, but for some reason the environment seemed more comfortable. This place was closer to home. Serious concentration, I thought, might just dissolve the obstacle between my situation and reality.

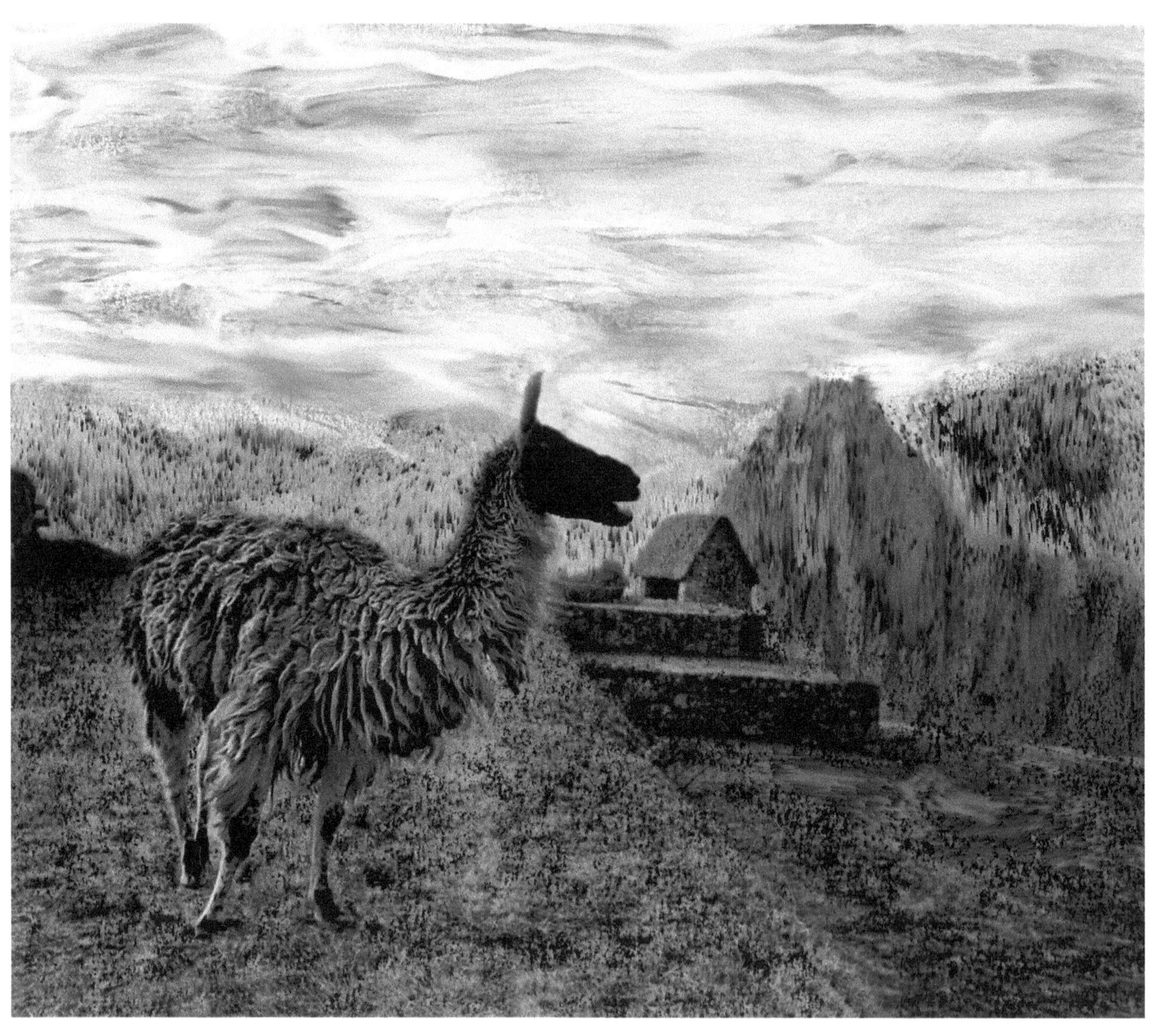

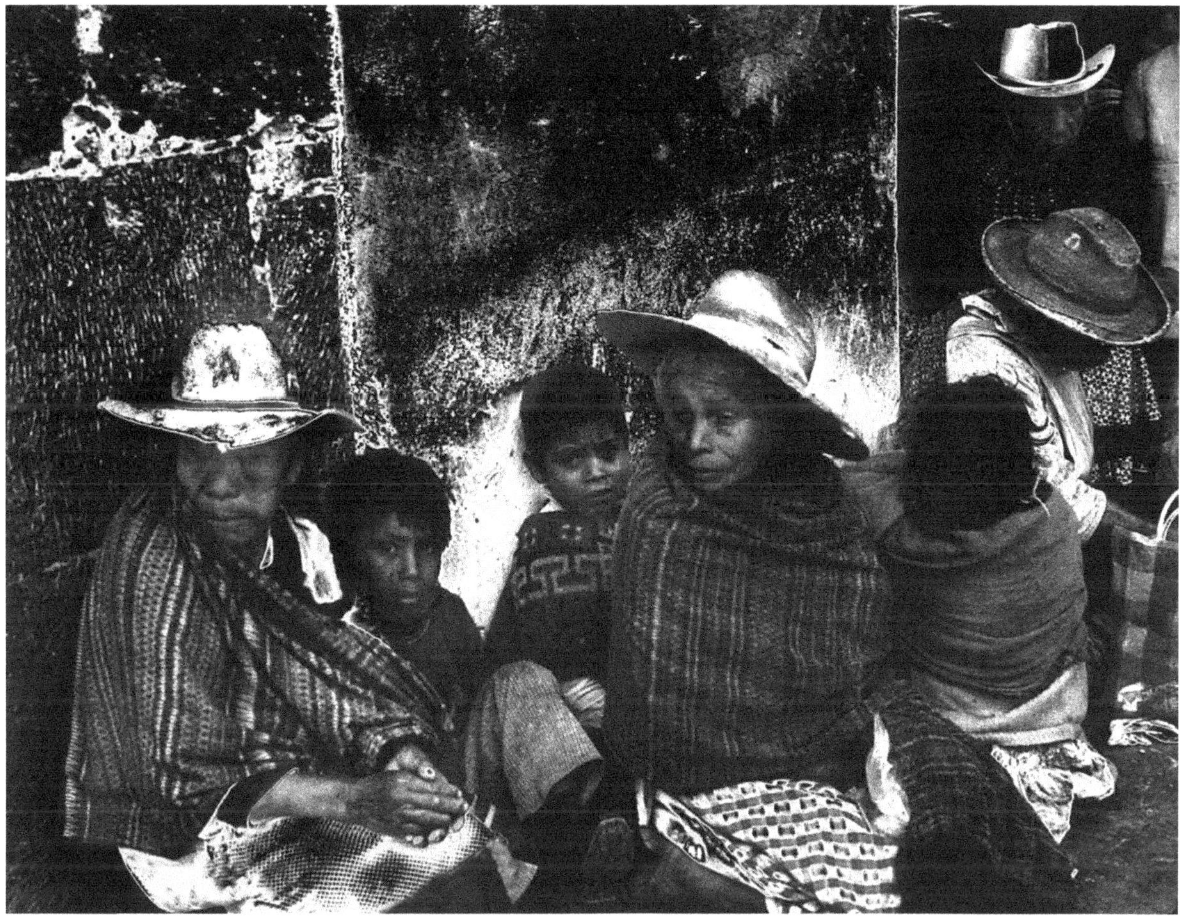

I was thinking about some recent dream incarnations when I realized I was in dream thought, very close to being lucid.

Lucid dreaming is the act of realizing you are in a dream. An accomplished lucid dreamer can direct and control the dream to, say, extract himself from a nightmare, or achieve some other goal, a practice I have never accomplished.

This was my chance. I looked around and realized my mind had carried me south of the border, to Mexico and probably farther, judging by the appearance of things.

I was just lucid enough to deduce that by traveling due south (at the speed of dreams), I could get back to where I started (what with the world being round, and all).

I was not lucid enough to realize that dream world abides by no such physical laws. In fact the rules change with the dream, and the one I was in worked on a flat, linear, multi-layered basis. And so I headed off into oblivion.

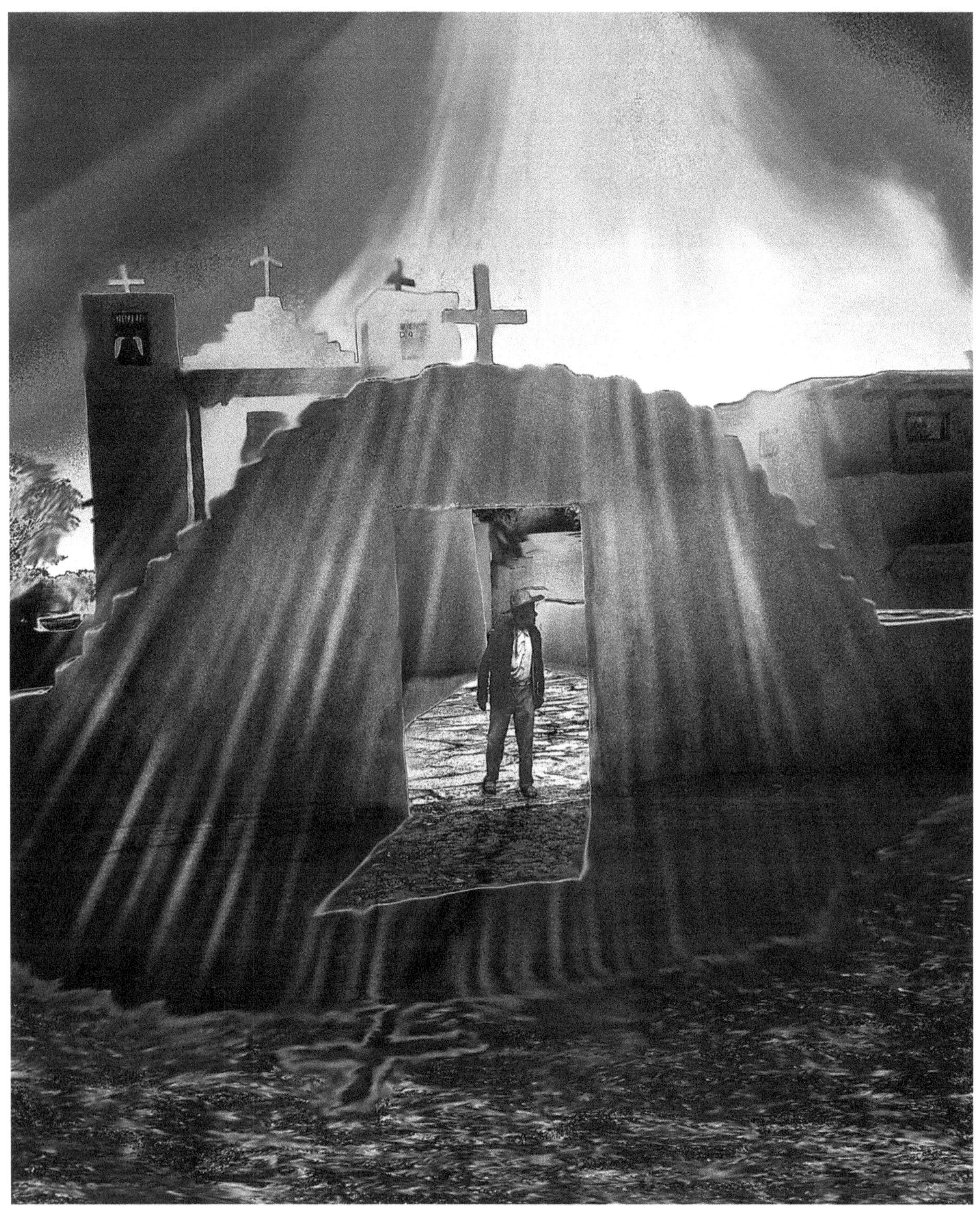

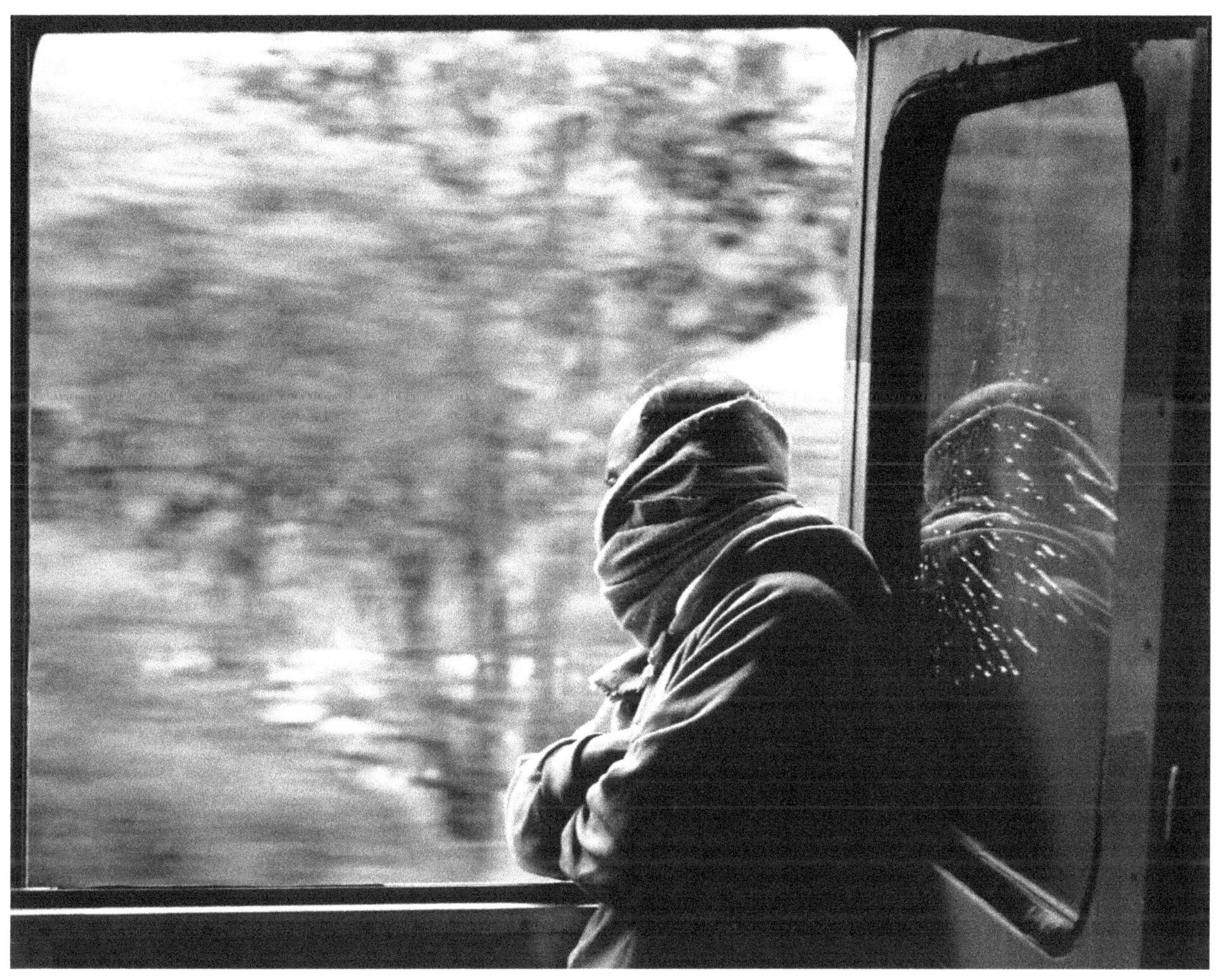

And then I was on a train that seemed to be speeding into yet another dream.

An interview with the Author, Jim McJunkin

by Carroll Wilson

CW: How did you get into photography?

JM: Originally I borrowed a Voigtlander camera with a range finder, which means you don't actually see what you get because you're not looking through the lens. I borrowed that from my dad. And I played around with it until I ruined it, and he never gave me another.

Actually, I got into art first. But I was having trouble coming up with ideas to paint. Later, I bought an old Minolta 35-millimeter, single-lens reflex, and I would just go out and take pictures of friends and then paint from those pictures. That worked okay, but I slowly evolved into a photographer. I was having more fun taking pictures than painting.

I was shooting black-and white because I couldn't afford color. That was when I was in high school. Then in college, I stuck with the art major and got a little better at painting, but I always came back to photography. I wasn't a good student. I was living in Denver, Colorado, but went to North Texas State University and eventually just walked out and went to New Orleans. I figured I could learn more about art in the French Quarter than in school.

CW: Well back then, back in the late 1960s, the United States had a draft, pulling young men into the military to serve in Vietnam. Didn't that worry you? You had to stay in college to keep out of the draft.

JM: I got incompletes in everything, and it was really hard to start over. The draft didn't enter my mind when I walked out. But when it did dawn on me, I got back into a junior college and once again didn't do well. I went on probation. I had to spend a semester out. One day I got a notice to go down to the recruitment office. So, that day, I signed up because I was told that if you signed up you got preferential treatment. That was not necessarily the case, but it worked out well for me.

The recruiting sergeant asked all sorts of questions, and then he asked about my profession. I had just seen a movie about a photographer who had sex with almost every girl he met, and I figured that would be good for me too, so I told the sergeant I was a professional photographer. He was skeptical, but he wrote it down. I'm the only guy I ever heard of that got what he lied about.

CW: Were you really aware of the war and anti-war sentiment?

JM: In Denver I took some pictures of antiwar demonstrators. It was a major happening, and I could tell big things were taking place. Streets were flooded with people. I took pictures of everything. I really wanted to document the whole thing. I don't really know why. I just knew it was strange, so I went out and took pictures of it.

CW: Did you save all those photos?

JM: I saved all my negatives. I got lucky too. I used to keep all my negatives in a metal ice chest, including my Vietnam negs. The house I was living in caught fire and almost all our possessions were destroyed. But thanks to the ice chest, I still have those negatives.

CW: So, you were a combat photographer in Vietnam in 1970. Please describe the experience.

JM: I had certain assignments I would be sent out on. Might be going down the Mekong River with a convoy of barges to pick up helicopter fuel, then delivering the fuel back upriver. The trip down river was a joy ride. Going back up, the barges were slow and full of fuel, which made them perfect targets for an ambush.

I also traveled with the 11th ACR quite a bit. I was really a documentarian. They wanted, the public information office, wanted just anything they considered Army—guys doing everyday stuff. Not just war. I had that Minolta, so I would take pictures for the Army and myself. I would turn the Army pictures in, and they eventually ended up in the Library of Congress. I kept my own negatives and sent them home in letters. I remember my first time out in the field. I was with the 11th Armored Cavalry, going through tunnels that had been bombed the night before. I didn't want to get off the tank. It took some prodding. After that I became bolder, almost to the point of stupidity.

Being a photographer with a press pass, I had more freedom than a lot of guys. Between assignments I would go out and catch a Vietnamese bus to some nearby village and wander around taking pictures. That seemed safe enough at the time, maybe because I wasn't in the jungle and there weren't any weapons involved. That was after some familiarity with being in-country. I was in a few firefights and those were frightening. For the most part, I was just bored.

CW: Do you ever want to go back to Vietnam and revisit those places?

JM: I want to go to Cambodia, and I'd kind of like to go to North Vietnam. At the time I was deathly afraid of Cambodia and North Vietnam because that's where the NVA (soldiers in the North Vietnamese Army) were coming from. I was always relieved to be farther south than north. Now that I've read more about the war during the time I was there, I realize I was mostly in the area the NVA were going to. Turned out I didn't know what was going on.

I have looked into going to Angkor Wat in Cambodia. The reason for that is I would like to see a civilization that existed so long ago. And the pictures I've seen of the jungle growing over those giant stone carvings are fascinating. Giant faces peering out of the jungle. I would not go back to Vietnam for nostalgic reasons. I don't want to relive any of that. I want to see what's happening now more than anything.

CW: What kind of camera gear do you carry today?
JM: I carry two cameras now. One is for black-and-white film. That's a holdover from the old days. And the other is digital. Both are made by Nikon. The digital camera is a D90. The black-and-white is a Nikon N80. And yes, you can still buy black-and-white film, although the chemistry to make the photographs is getting hard to find.

CW: I would have thought digital produced far better quality than something like TriX black-and-white.

JM: There used to be a big difference between digital and film. I don't think that is the case anymore but it seems to me that you get more shades of grey from a well exposed frame of film. Also, I believe film still holds the archival edge. Those gaps are narrowing too, since the digital image keeps evolving while the darkroom image seems stagnant. My D90 is the first camera I reach for these days, but I'm still not ready to cut the other one loose.

CW: Do you ever shoot video?

JM: I have thought about it. And as an art major I did some. I've been driving down Ranch Road 12 in the late afternoon when the sun is coming through the trees and it's light, dark, light, dark, flashing, and that would make a great video. But, I never have done anything with it. I doubt I ever will. I will stick with what I know.

CW: In reference to the kind of work that appears in this book, where do you come up with ideas for your subjects?

JM: First of all, the type of work that is in the book—95 percent of it or more—are things that really didn't work out for me in the first place. They were good, maybe really good pictures, but there was something lacking, and they were not going into my portfolio because they were not as good as I could do. So, when I have shots like that I'll stick them up on the bulletin board and look at them for a while to see what they need. I might see something I can do, so I will digitize them and put them into Photoshop.

Now I would never do that with my Vietnam portfolio, or any documentary images. Documentary portfolios are in a separate category. Most anything else, I'll put up on the board and play with it. Once, I tried what is called selective development on a portrait that I thought could use a little help. I exposed the paper under my enlarger, but instead of immersing it in developer, I soaked a cotton swab in developer and rubbed it over the area where the eyes and lips would be. That was kind of cool, but eyes and lips on a white background still didn't do the trick, so I did it again and then sprayed the whole print with developer from a spray bottle. That made eyes and lips and little black dots in places the developer landed on the print. I did that whole process again on another sheet of paper, and spun it horizontally, which made squiggles instead of dots. About twenty prints later I made an image I liked. Lips, eyes, streaks of hair, and squiggles. The darkroom was a mess.

CW: When did you begin the kind of photography that is in this book?

JM: Ever since I had a darkroom, I have put images on a bulletin board, and then embellished them by cutting and pasting. I didn't have my own darkroom until I got out of the Army and got my own apartment. I set my enlarger up in the kitchen, or a closet, anyplace I could make dark enough. I always wanted to paint on photographs, but they always ended up looking like photographs that were painted.

I never got decent results until I think I just got frustrated and started slapping paint on. When the acrylic was almost dry, I would gently wipe it with a wet sponge. Some of that paint came off, and some of it stuck. I would wipe all the paint off outside the contours—say the arms and legs, if it was a photo of a body. Wait until the paint dries, then repeat the process over and over until you have a multi-layered masterpiece, or something worthy of the trashcan. Actually, that method works best with resin coated paper, so if the end result is a disaster, (and many of them are), you can put the print in a tray of warm water, and the paint will slide off. Hang it up to dry and try again.

CW: Did you ever think about a career in photography?

JM: The closest I came to having a career involved strippers. That was over forty years ago, when they traveled around the country and needed promotional shots. Some of the girls had special acts. I did a portfolio of a stripper who danced with snakes and tarantulas. I knew someone who booked these women for a club in Austin. She called me up one day and said she had a girl who needed publicity pictures. They worked out great. That was something I enjoyed doing, and the closest I came to having a job in photography. Then I met (my wife) Beth and that came to a screeching halt.

CW: Do you have a favorite photo in the book?

JM: My favorite is the picture of my wife and the dog's legs under water. It was taken with an old Nikonos camera. The thing is ancient, an underwater camera. No light meter, and no real view-finder to speak of. You have to guess at exposure and focus, and composition. I got into underwater photography for a few years and hardly did anything but that. So I have a ton of underwater pictures too. What made that picture special is I got it right. Not just the legs, but the reflections and light. It all got captured on film. I didn't think it was special until I saw the contact sheet.

That is something great about photography—the pleasant surprises. You know there is something there, or you would not have taken the shot in the first place. Then you see the image as a print, and there are all those subtle things going on in the background, or visual lines that lead you into the picture. There is a lot going on in that underwater image that did not seem as important in real time. I'm sure I saw the reflections, but I thought the legs were the story.

CW: Do you have favorite places to photograph?

JM: My favorite place is some place I've never been before. There are lots of places I have returned to. Lake Powell (Utah) is one of them. When I go to someplace strange, and see things I don't normally see, I take more pictures. It's easier to see a picture in somebody else's back yard.

CW: How many photos do you take in a typical session? And from that, how many will you choose to work with?

JM: I take hundreds of pictures with my digital camera. If I see something I like, I shoot the hell out of it. My wife and I just got back from a trip to Europe. We were gone three weeks. I shot 14 rolls of 36-exposure black-and-white film. Also over 1,000 digital images. And I got exactly three that I will use in the portfolio. Those numbers will probably change, especially if I end up manipulating some of them. Still, my percentages aren't very good.

CW: You have photos other than the ones in the book, obviously. What plans do you have for them?

JM: I don't know that I have any plans. I just take pictures and save them. I put them in my portfolio and hope someday I can do something with them. Since I started this book, and found somebody interested in it, I'm starting to think, Oh, I'll do another on travel, or being stuck in a dream while traveling.

I'm beginning to think about all the images I have stashed away in a closet. Some of those negatives, and Kodachromes haven't seen the light of day for forty years. Basically, what I do right now, I'm in the Wimberley Valley Art League, and once every six weeks I submit pictures for possible inclusion in the next show they sponsor. That sort of keeps me interested and making prints.

CW: Do you really have a lot of dreams?

JM: Yes. I really do. A lot of them are kind of boring dreams. I actually still dream a lot about work, and I retired over six years ago. I used to be a cable splicer for the phone company. For some reason I still dream about putting fiber optics together.

Every once in a while I will have a dream that really stands out, and I'll write it down. I have a collection of little slips of paper with dreams written on them. That collection goes way back, and I still have a notepad in the drawer by my bed for that purpose. Some of those dreams made it into the book. My flying dream was real, and so was the dream about the kids' teeth melting. I have plenty of real dreams to work with, but for the book, I had trouble coming up with pictures to fit my dreams, so I made up some dreams to fit my pictures.

www.ingramcontent.com/pod-product-compliance
Lightning Source LLC
LaVergne TN
LVHW060627110826
845147LV00015B/954

* 9 7 8 1 9 4 2 9 5 6 0 4 4 *